Penguin Handbooks

Simple Clothes and How to Make Them

Kerstin Lokrantz was born in Stockholm in 1928 and went to the Otte Sköld School of Painting and the Anders Beckman School for Advertising and Fashion Designers. She now teaches clothes design at the Anders Beckman School and at the Swedish State School of Arts, Crafts and Design. From 1950 to 1970 she worked, designing clothes, for the Swedish clothing industry and has also designed, on a freelance basis, for the older age-groups and for working people in various professions. In addition she has written magazine articles, radio programmes and books about clothes and their history.

KERSTIN LOKRANTZ

SIMPLE CLOTHES AND HOW TO MAKE THEM

Translated from the Swedish by
Päivi Crofts

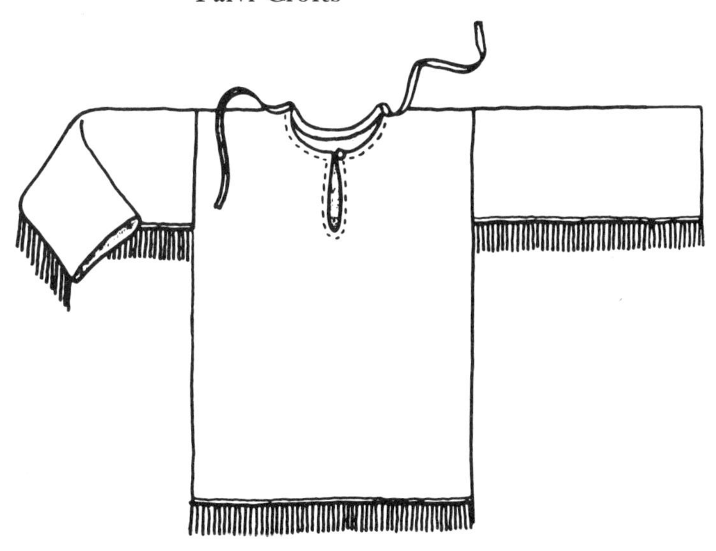

PENGUIN BOOKS

Penguin Books Ltd, Harmondsworth,
Middlesex, England
Penguin Books, 625 Madison Avenue,
New York, New York 10022, U.S.A.
Penguin Books Australia Ltd, Ringwood,
Victoria, Australia
Penguin Books Canada Ltd, 2801 John Street,
Markham, Ontario, Canada, L3R 1B4
Penguin Books (N.Z.) Ltd, 182–190 Wairau Road,
Auckland 10, New Zealand

This book consists of selections from two Swedish books:
Enkla kläder som man kan sy själo,
first published by Bokförlaget Prisma, 1972
(copyright © Kerstin Lokrantz, 1972) and
Nya enkla kläder för barn och vuxna,
first published by Bokförlaget Prisma, 1975
(copyright © Kerstin Lokrantz, 1975).

This selection first published 1978

Patterns drawn by Gun Jonasson

Made and printed in Great Britain by
Butler & Tanner Ltd, Frome and London

Contents

Preface

In many parts of the world there are garments whose design has remained unchanged for generations, worn alongside commercial fashion. This traditional clothing made by the people for themselves has a robust and simple charm of its own, and can be very beautiful. I have taken thirty such garments, some of which are wonderfully easy to make – for example the ruana from Colombia – even for beginners who have had little experience with the sewing machine.

Even the cutting of these clothes does not demand any great amount of skill. Small mistakes will not spoil the final product.

Many of the garments described can be worn by men or women, adults or children. For some styles I have made suggestions for further refinements; but my main aim is that these patterns may be used as a basis for your own ideas. The character of these clothes is, of course, greatly influenced by the kind of material you use. If you make the same design out of different materials, you may end up with several garments which are all very different.

At the beginning of the book, on pp. 11–18, there is a section of general notes giving advice on how to use the patterns, how to adapt them to your size and shape, how to do various seams and bindings suggested in the text, and so on. I would recommend all readers to have a look at this section before starting on a pattern.

Acknowledgements

The publishers wish to thank the following for their kind permission to reproduce photographs:
Per B. Adolphson (p. 138); Sten Didrik Bellander (p. 72); Hans Eriksson (p. 83); Försvarsstabens pressdetalj (p. 130); Bengt af Geijerstam (p. 70); Sven Gillsäter (p. 61); Rune Hassner (p. 97 left); Tore Johnson (p. 59); Anita Lundberg (p. 143); Pål Nils Nilson (p. 51); Nordiska museet (pp. 36, 77, 88, 127 and 157); George Oddner (p. 115); Lennart Pettersson (p. 97 right); Svenska filminstitutet, Filmhistorika samlingarna (p. 120); Der wilde Westen, Urs Graf-Verlag (p. 103); Etnografiska museet, Stockholm, 47.

How to use the patterns

Scale on the patterns

As you will see, all the patterns are marked 'Scale 1:10' or 'Scale 1:5'.

Scale 1: 10 means that every millimetre – i.e. every little square – on the diagram is one centimetre on the pattern. All measurements on the diagram are therefore multiplied by 10, e.g. 27 mm means 27 cm.

Scale 1: 5 means that every millimetre on the diagram is 5 millimetres (or half a centimetre) on the pattern; and every centimetre 5 centimetres. So all measurements must be multiplied by 5, for example 10 mm=5 cm.

Most of the measurements have been worked out already and are marked in centimetres on the diagrams. Where they are not you simply count the millimetre squares and multiply by 10 or 5.

Sizes

Very few of the garments in this book fit closely and the women's garments should fit most women between sizes 10 and 14. The patterns are basically drawn for a women's size 12 and men's size 40–42 inch chest. Because most of the garments are loose fitting the width of the *garment*, rather than the size of the *wearer*, is given on many of the patterns. The centre-back length is given too. On children's patterns the height of the child is given, as a child's age is often a poor indication of its size.

Measuring yourself

Here are the standard measurements in centimetres:

Size	8	10	12	14	16
Bust	80	83	87	92	97
Waist	61	64	67	71	76
Hip	85	88	92	97	102

In checking your size with the above table or with a particular pattern, these points should be borne in mind:

Waist: When measuring the waist, do not draw the tape measure unnaturally tight, or leave it too loose; hold it snug around the body just above the hips.

Hip: Measure the largest point of your hips: let the tape measure slide up and down over the hips to make sure the garment will go over them.

Bust: Measure the largest point of your bust.

Outside leg: Measure from the waist down the outside of the leg to the foot. This should be done before finalizing the length of trouser legs.

Before cutting a garment, also measure your arm and leg lengths, as these vary a lot from person to person, even if the people are the same 'size'.

Adapting patterns to your size

To *increase* the pattern one size, add 2·5 centimetres to the breadth back and front; that is, add one centimetre on each side and half a centimetre (5 mm) in the middle to the back and the front. Raise the shoulder by half a centimetre on each side. If you want to increase the pattern by *two* sizes you will have to double the increases already given, and also make the shoulder seam half a centimetre wider at the

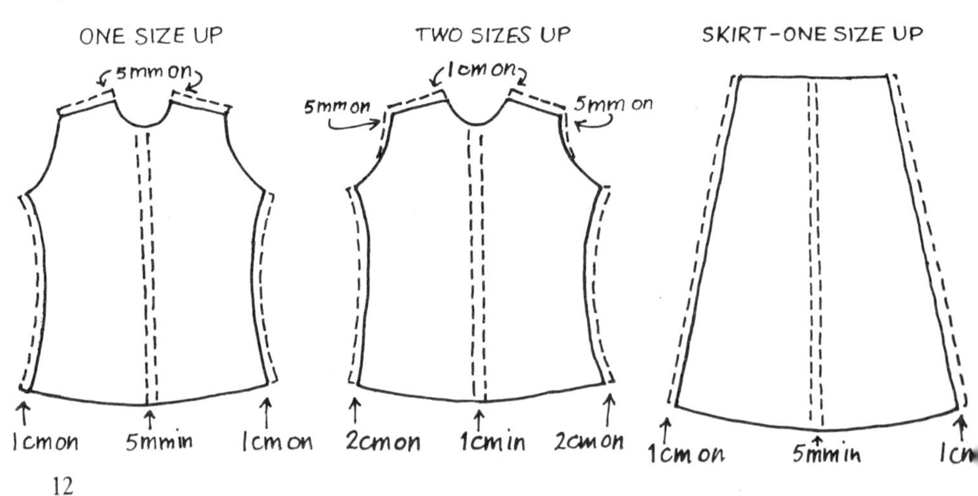

armhole edge. Add to trousers on the outside seams only, not on the inside leg or crotch. It is sometimes better to add extra length to a skirt at the waist rather than the hem, so as not to spoil the flare (see the flared skirt, p. 76).

To *decrease* the pattern one size, subtract 2·5 centimetres from all measurements, in the same places as the increases described above.

If your waist is very small take larger darts at the waist running further down the skirt. Or take in more on the seams at the top of the skirt, sloping gently into the already slanting seams. If you have a large bust for your size, allow extra width at the bust and then take off from the centre back, centre front or side seams, or all of these.

Seam allowances

Seam allowances are given with each set of instructions and must be *added on* to the basic measurement, *before* cutting.

Pattern paper

1. This can be bought in shops. In England it is usually dotted and crossed by the inch. You can also buy plain paper and draw the squares yourself. Any large piece of paper will do, even newspaper.
2. Use transparent paper and pin it over a sheet of squared paper. The squared paper can then be used again for other patterns.
3. Buy a pattern board. These cost about £2–£4, but they show squares in inches and centimetres and give the bias line. They measure about six feet by four feet and fold up. Very useful.

If your paper is not large enough for a whole pattern piece, sellotape two or more sheets together.

Transferring the pattern marks to the fabric

Pattern marks have to be transferred from the pattern on to the fabric – for instance, position of pockets, darts, pleats, pin tucks, centre front and centre back. You can do this with dressmaker's carbon paper – a spiked wheel transfers marks to the cloth. To do this place the carbon paper face down between the pattern and the wrong side of the fabric.

Or you can use tailor's chalk, which comes in a flat disc and makes nice, fine marks that can be rubbed off afterwards; or you can simply use tailor's tacks. All markings should be made on the wrong side of the fabric so that they are consistent and you can see what you are doing when you sew.

How much fabric?

All the patterns give the length of fabric required – in some cases with varying widths. (For a metric/imperial conversion table, see p. 171.) If you make changes of size in the pattern check the fabric required by cutting out the pattern before buying the fabric. Don't forget seam allowances. If you use a different width of fabric, make sure that pieces intended to be cut on the straight or bias are still cut in this way.

Nap and patterned fabric

If you are sewing with velvet, corduroy, velour or other fabrics which have a nap going one way you will have to arrange the pattern layout so that all the pieces lie in the same direction on the fabric – otherwise the colour may appear to vary. The best way to test whether nap will cause a problem is to cut a small slip of fabric from the end of the roll in the shop, lay it on the fabric with the nap going in the opposite direction and see whether there is any difference in colour (but be sure that the lighting is good). If there is a difference in colour you will have to adapt the pattern layout so that the pieces all lie in the same direction – you may have to buy extra fabric to allow for this (see, for example, the flared skirt on p. 76). If in doubt ask the sales people.

Stripes, checks and large patterns need similar care. To make sure that they match on adjoining seams, lay your paper pattern out on the fabric and mark in pencil on the pattern edge where the stripes, checks, and so on, come. You can then match up the pattern pieces when cutting out.

Seams

French seam

Sew the seam with the wrong sides together and a seam allowance of 1·5 cm on both sides. Trim the seam allowances down to 5 mm or even less with fine fabrics. Turn the garment so that the right sides are together and sew the seam again, 7 mm from the edge, or as close to the previous seam as possible while making sure that the raw edges are hidden inside the seam. This makes a neat, secure seam which doesn't need finishing.

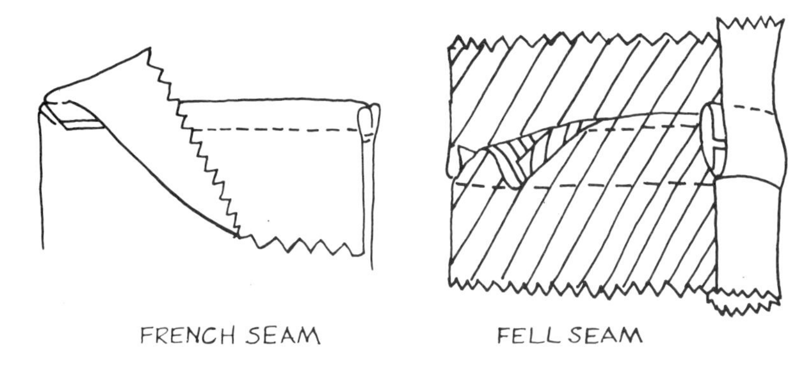

FRENCH SEAM FELL SEAM

Fell seam

Lay the two pieces of material right sides facing each other. Sew 1·5 cm from the edge. Trim one of the seam allowances down to 7 mm. Press the larger seam allowance over the narrower one, fold in the edge and sew along the fold, about 1 cm from the first seam. This seam needs no further finishing.

Curved seams

You may have to clip a curved seam – at the neck or armhole, for example – in order to make it lie flat. Clip the turnings neatly, but not quite, down to the seam line at 1·5 cm intervals round the curve.

Finishing seams

Other seams can be finished with a zigzag or overlocking stitch on a machine, or oversewn by hand.

Bound edges

To make bias binding

Cut a bias or crosswise strip out of the cloth as follows:

1. Lay the cloth in a triangle so that the two selvedges are at right angles to each other.

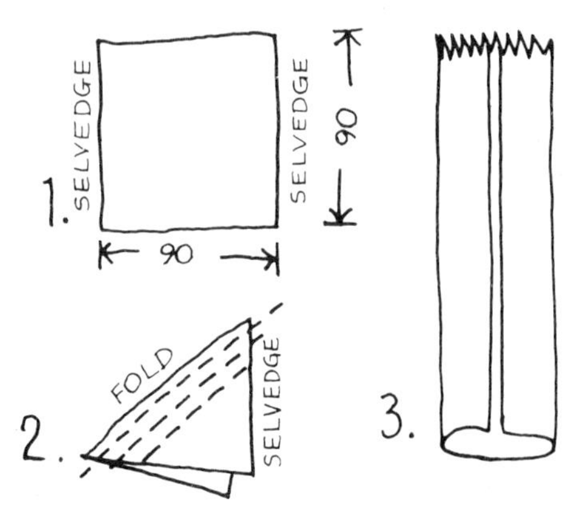

2. Cut along the folded side of the triangle thus formed, about 1·5 cm from the fold.
3. Press in 1 cm on both sides of the strip. This strip is on the bias of the cloth and will stretch to fit curves and corners.

You can buy ready-made bias binding but it is not always of very good quality. If the garment is made in thick material it is best to use home-made bindings. If you are binding a straight edge you can use ribbon or braid, but these are not suitable for curved edges as they are not cut on the bias and will not stretch.

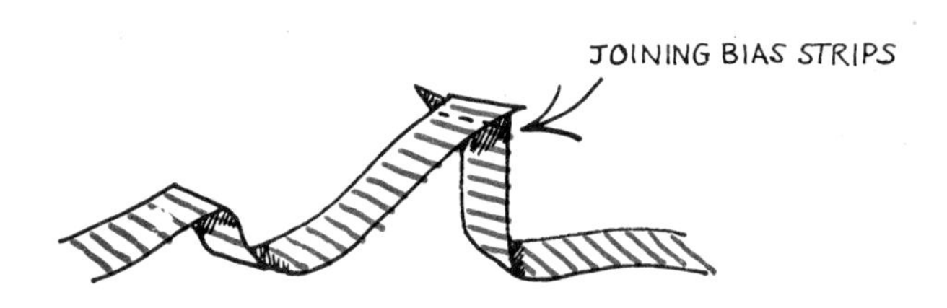

To use bias binding

Open out one fold of the binding and lay the binding right side down on the inside of the garment at the edge. Sew along the fold line. Turn the binding over to the right side of the garment and sew the binding down on the right side, sewing as close as you can to the folded edge.

If you are binding a neck or armhole you can stretch the bias binding a little to make a good curve. If the neck or armhole is a bit too large, you can take in some of the extra width by stretching the bias binding. When binding straight edges or hems, do not stretch the binding at all.

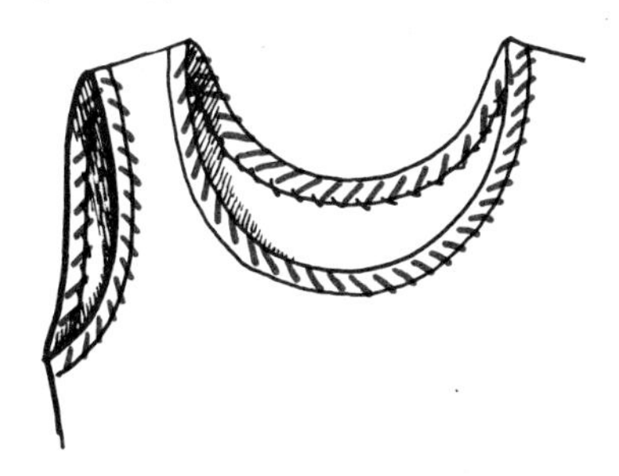

Belts, bands and ties

To make these fold the strip of material in half lengthways, right sides together. Sew along the edge and then turn it right side out by pulling one end through the channel thus formed. Seam both ends.

Sleeve with gusset

Many of the patterns in this book require a gusset to be inserted under the arm. This is done to give greater movement in the sleeve. You sew a gusset in as follows:

1. Mark the sleeve and gusset with the letters ABCD.
2. Stitch together the gusset and sleeve so that A on one corresponds with A on the other.

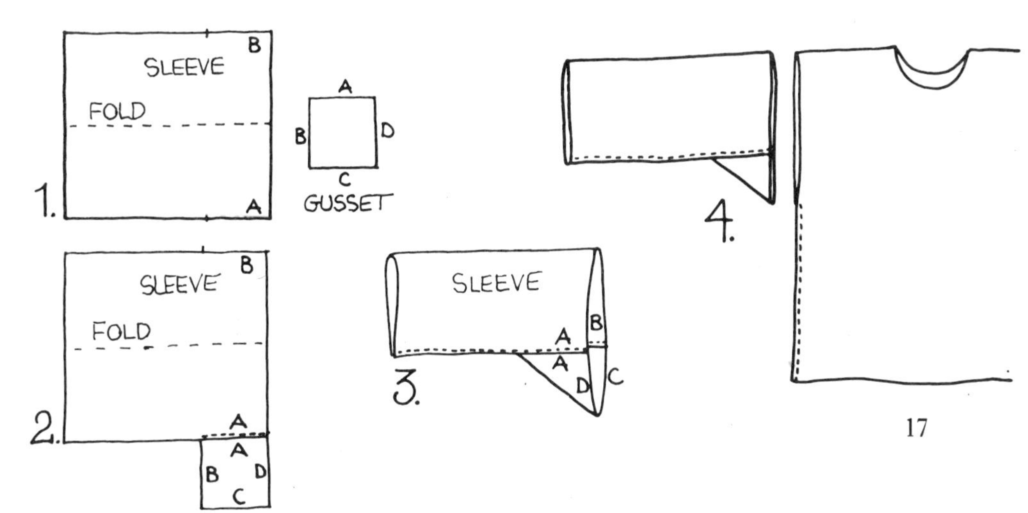

3. Stitch the sleeve seam together towards the gusset so that B on the arm is joined to B on the gusset.
4. Pin the sleeve to the body of the garment, the side seam of which has already been stitched together up to the marking for the gusset. The point of the gusset between C and D must join the side seam of the garment.

Before buying the material – checklist

If you alter the pattern in any way, or if your material comes in a different width from that given in the instructions, you will have to adjust the length of the material which you need to buy. The following checklist is a reminder of all the points you will have to consider when deciding how much material to buy.

1. Check your measurements and decide whether you will have to alter the pattern to fit you (see p. 11). Even if the garment is the right size you may want to adjust the length or the sleeve length. Most of these garments are loose fitting and will fit a range of sizes.
2. Remember to add on the seam allowance given with each pattern.
3. If you need to alter the pattern at all make a rough diagram giving all the new measurements and the seam allowances too.
4. Check that your pattern pieces will still fit on the material, and adapt the layout if necessary.
5. Check whether you have to allow extra material for matching stripes, checks or large patterns (see p. 14), or because the material has a nap (see p. 14).
6. Check whether your material comes in the stated width. If it does not you will have to adapt the pattern layout (you can do this by cutting out the pieces in paper first), making sure that you cut on the straight of the fabric if this is shown in the original layout and use the same folds.
7. Check whether you will need more, or less, of the accessories – buttons, bias binding, and so on.

Before cutting, remember to add on the seam allowances given in the pattern instructions all round each piece.

The patterns

Artist's smock

The Swedish painter Carl Larsson was a practical man who used to make serviceable and attractive everyday clothes for his whole family. He himself wore very roomy artist's smocks of different lengths, made from bleached or unbleached cottons, with a colourful tie at the neck. Sometimes he added embroidery at the points of the collars.

The artist's smock can be worn by men or women as a cover-up for light work. The most suitable fabric is lightweight coloured or white cotton.

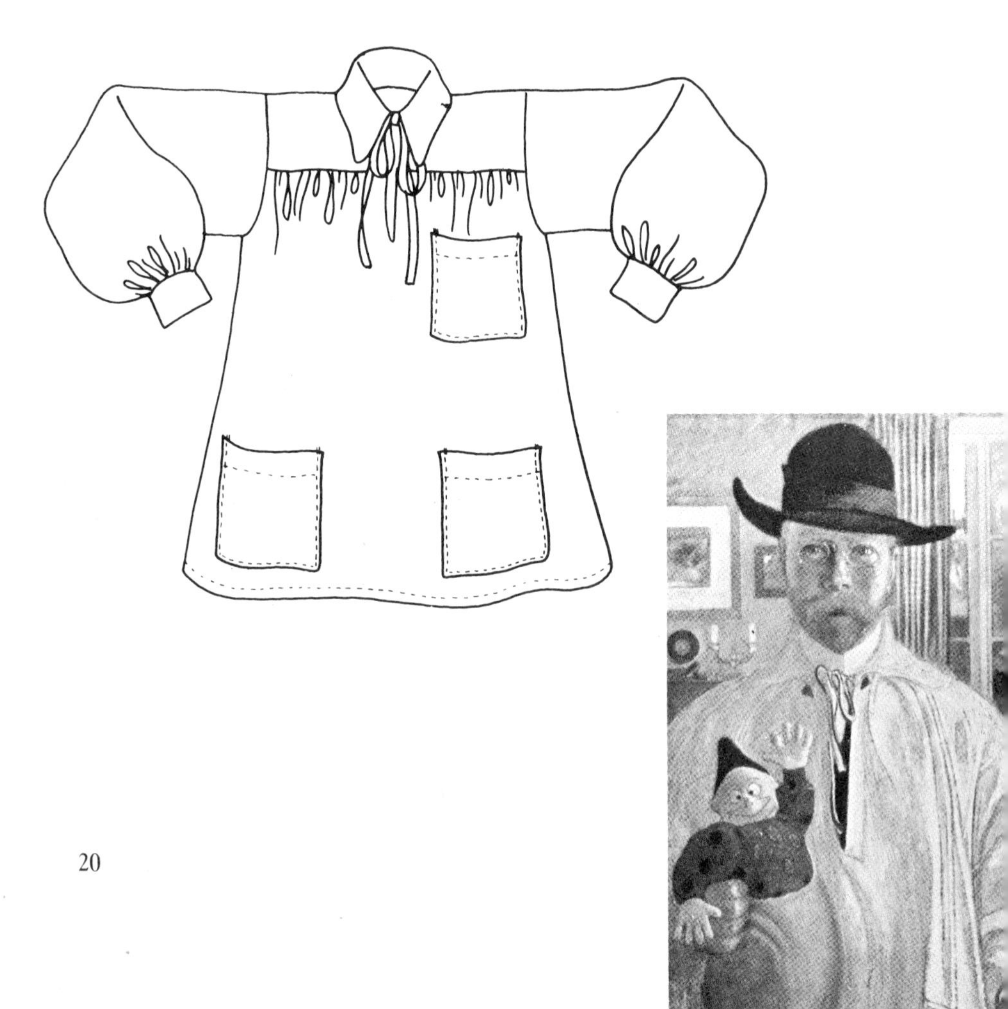

Instructions
Artist's smock

Material required:·210 × 140 cm or 340 × 90 cm; two buttons.
Seam allowance: 2 cm all round.

Fold in the seam allowance on the pockets. Press. Tack to the front as marked. Top-stitch close to the edge of the pocket. Press.

Gather the front and back pieces. Place the neck facing on the front, right sides together. Sew round the opening, cut the slash and turn the facing to the inside. Press. Fold under the wide turning on the bottom of the front and back yoke pieces and tack them to the front and back pieces. Top-stitch 2 cm from the edge. This makes a tuck over the gathers.

Sew the shoulder seams together. Sew and turn the collar and cuffs. Attach the collar. Sew up the sleeve seams, leaving a small opening at the wrist, which should be hemmed. Gather the wrists and adjust to fit the wristbands. Fold wristbands in half lengthwise, right sides together, and sew across the ends. Turn right side out and press. Pin one edge of the wristband to the sleeve, right sides together and sew. Turn the wristband to the inside, turn in the sleeve allowance, and slip-stitch over the seam on the inside. Sew the side seams. Sew in the sleeves. Make a buttonhole in each wristband as shown on the pattern, and sew on the buttons. Turn up and sew the hem. Sew ties at the neck to make a bow.

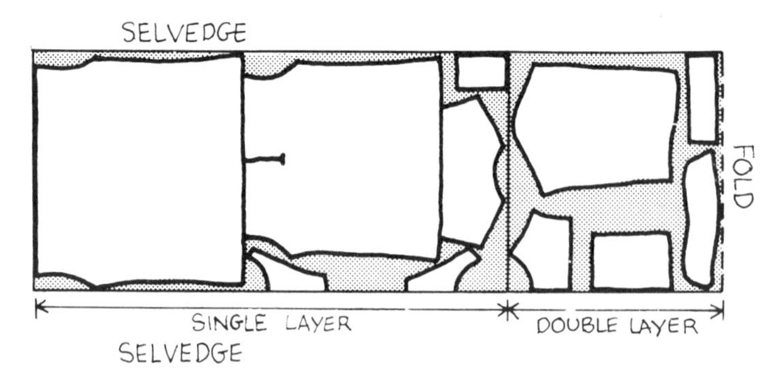

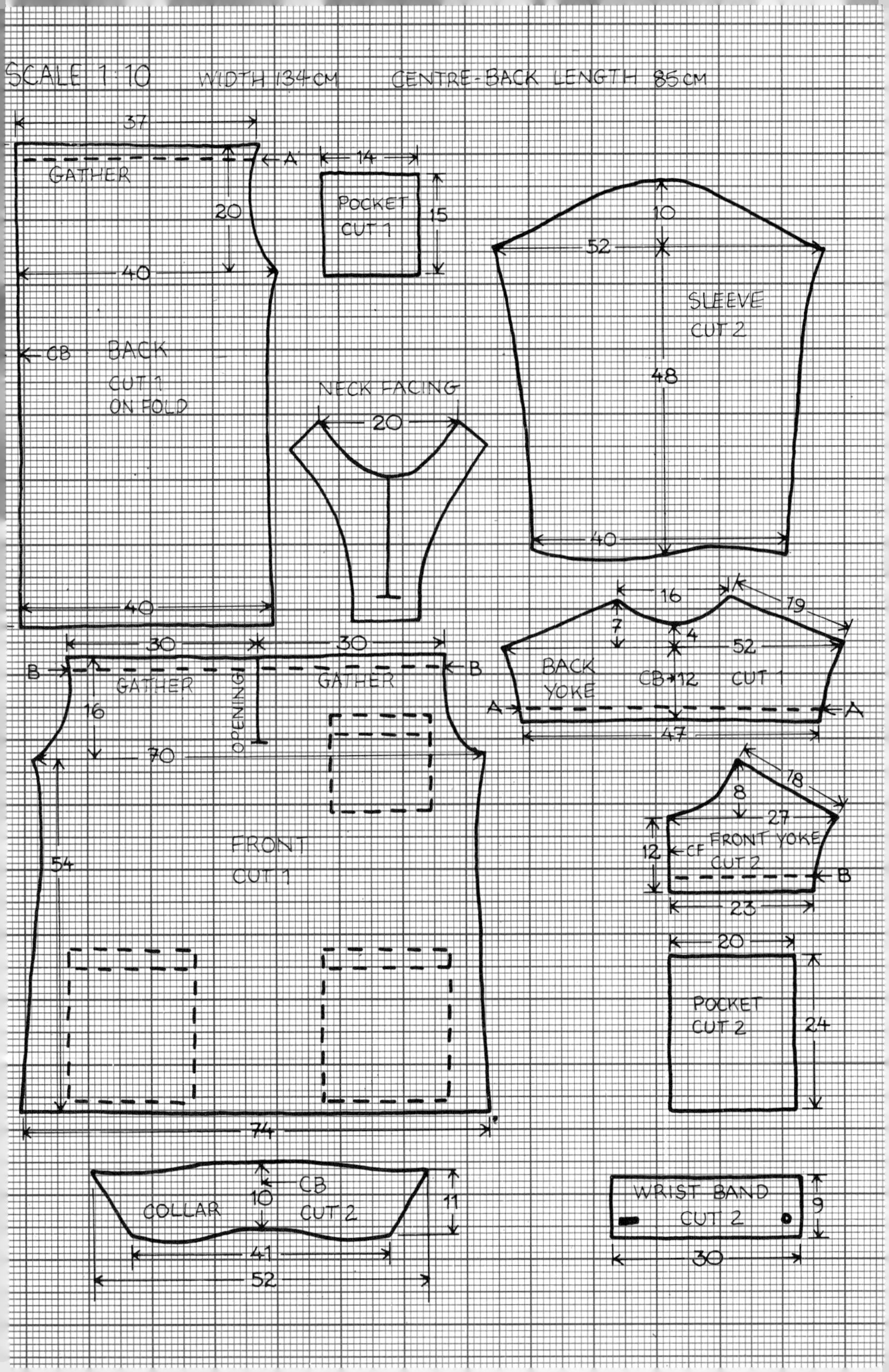

SCALE 1:10
WIDTH 134 CM
CENTRE-BACK LENGTH 85 CM
37
A
GATHER
20
40
CB
BACK
CUT 1
ON FOLD
40
14
POCKET
CUT 1
15
NECK FACING
20
10
52
SLEEVE
CUT 2
48
40
16
19
7
4
52
BACK
YOKE
CB
12
CUT 1
A
A
47
30
30
B
B
GATHER
OPENING
GATHER
16
70
54
FRONT
CUT 1
18
8
27
12
CF
FRONT YOKE
CUT 2
B
23
20
POCKET
CUT 2
24
74
CB
COLLAR
10
CUT 2
11
41
52
WRIST BAND
CUT 2
9
30

Sailor shirt

By the eighteenth century there were special shops where seamen could fit themselves out with ready-made shirts. In the Swedish navy this garment was called a blue-shirt and the sailors themselves modified the design of these working clothes. Naval rule prescribed that the shirt should be long and tucked into the trousers: but the cloth was rough and the arrangement clumsy. Despite the risk of punishment, therefore, the sailors began cutting off the bottom of the shirt so that it became a quite short, loose-hanging smock. This style was officially adopted around 1915 and the garment made thereafter as a very short blouse.

The sailor collar has a long history as an ornament, while the handkerchief had a practical use from the start as a rag to dry the man's eyes when the sweat was running. In the nineteenth century the sailor suit became both a playsuit and a Sunday costume for children of all classes, and the fashion survived until the 1930s.

The sailor shirt in the illustration is cut in the same way as the sailor shirt of the turn of the century, much shorter and intended to be worn outside the trousers. The handkerchief has been left out and the collar is made of the same fabric as the rest of the shirt. Suitable materials are some strong wools and Manchester or cotton twills.

Instructions
Sailor shirt

Material required: man's size, 200 × 140 cm; child's size, 115 × 90 cm; decorative braid.
Seam allowance: 2 cm all round.

Lay the pattern pieces on the cloth, mark the seam allowances all around each piece and cut them out.

Put the front and the back of the shirt together, right sides together, and sew the shoulder seams. Finish off the seams and press them open.

Right sides together, stitch the collar to the collar facing round the outer edges. Turn the collar right side out and press. Tack on decorative braid and sew.

Tack in the sleeves, sew them on and finish off the seams. Sew the sleeve and side seams in one go ending the side seams at the top of the openings.

Tack the collar firmly to the right side of the shirt on the neckline. Adjust the neck if necessary. Finish off the seams. Fold up the wide cuffs and sew. Cover this seam with braid sewn on the right side of the sleeve.

Sew the shoulder seams of the facings and press them open. Finish off the outer edge of the facing. Lay the facing on the collar, right sides together, and sew it to the neckline. Turn the facing down and press. Straighten the collar, sew a row of stitching from the right side 2 mm away from the neckline to hold the facing in place. Fasten the facing to the shoulder seams by hand.

Hem the top of the pocket. Cover the seam with braid sewn on the right side. Press in the seam allowances of the three other sides, and tack the pocket to the shirt as marked on the pattern. Sew close to the edge of the pocket.

Hem the shirt. Sew around both sides of the openings evenly. Press the shirt. Tie a bow of braid or a band of cloth and sew it on securely in the centre-front opening.

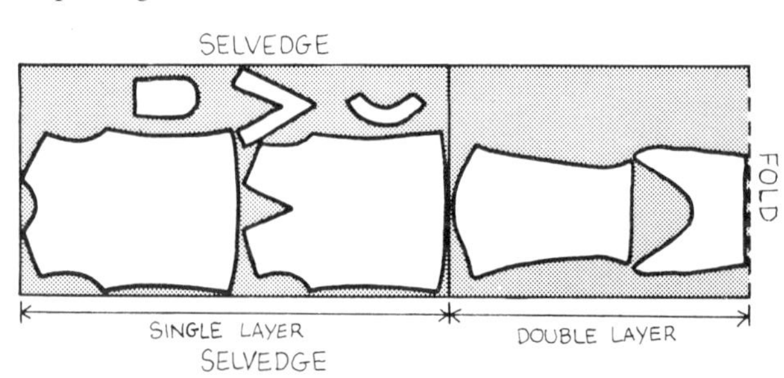

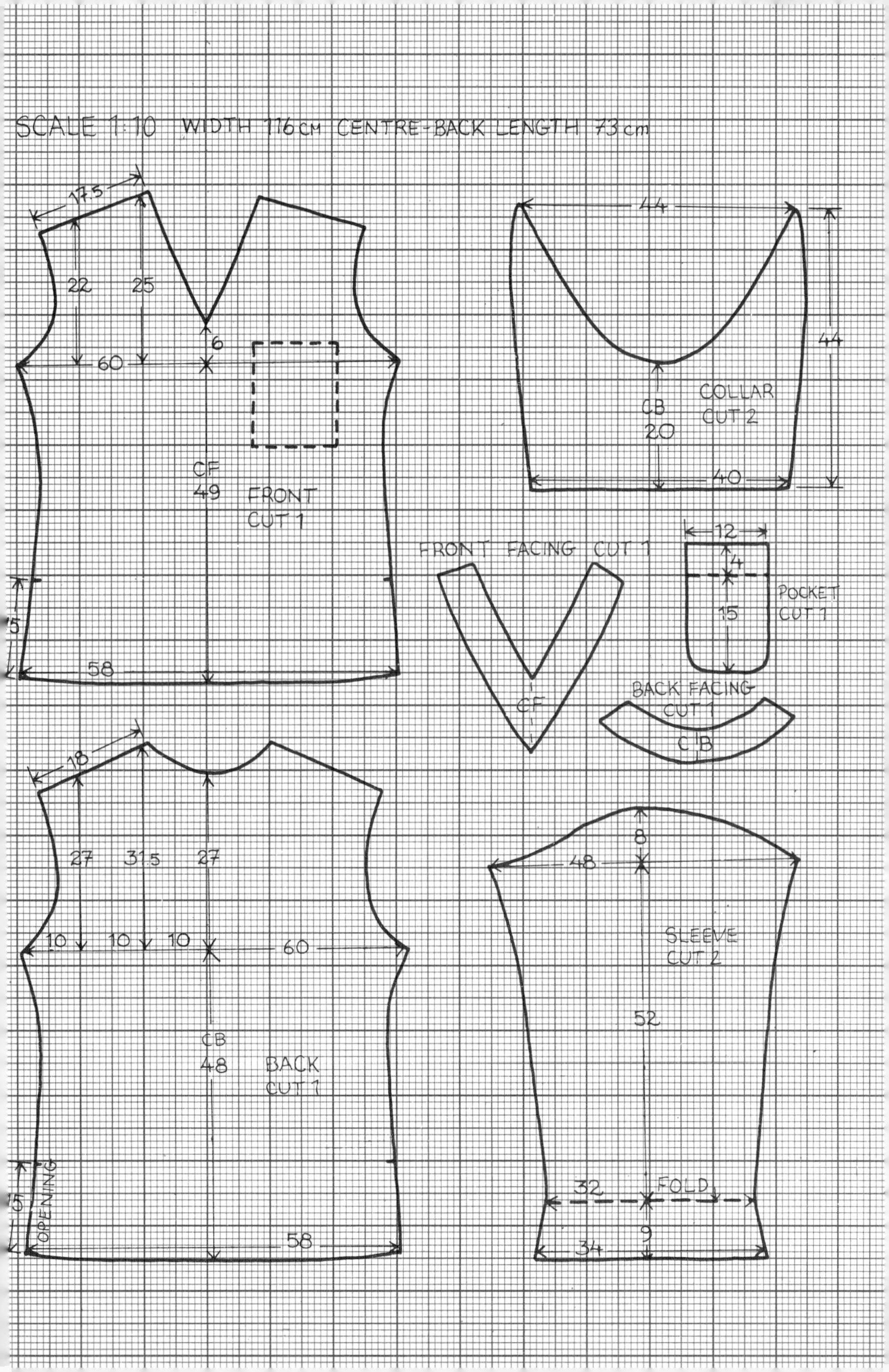

SCALE 1:10 WIDTH 116cm CENTRE-BACK LENGTH 73cm
17.5
22
25
6
60
CF
49
FRONT
CUT 1
15
58
44
44
COLLAR
CUT 2
CB
20
40
FRONT FACING CUT 1
CF
12
4
15
POCKET
CUT 1
BACK FACING
CUT 1
CB
18
27
31.5
27
10
10
10
60
CB
48
BACK
CUT 1
15
OPENING
58
8
48
SLEEVE
CUT 2
52
32
FOLD
9
34

Kimono

The kimono was introduced into Japan from China around AD 700. Like the kaftan, it is a coat with wide arms. It is much the same for men or women, for all ages and social classes, for winter and summer wear.

The garment is open in the front, has no buttons or hooks, but is held together with a sash, which is very wide for women. It is made of silk, and in cold weather people wear several, often as many as ten or more, for warmth. The upper layers are made with progressively shorter sleeves and wider neck openings, culminating in a sleeveless waistcoat so as to give maximum freedom of movement.

The kimono can be made either in cotton and worn as a housecoat, or in silk or fine cotton for going out, and may reach either to the knee or the floor. It also goes well over trousers. Two different fabrics may be combined in the same garment. The sash is so long that it can be wound round several times and tied at the back.

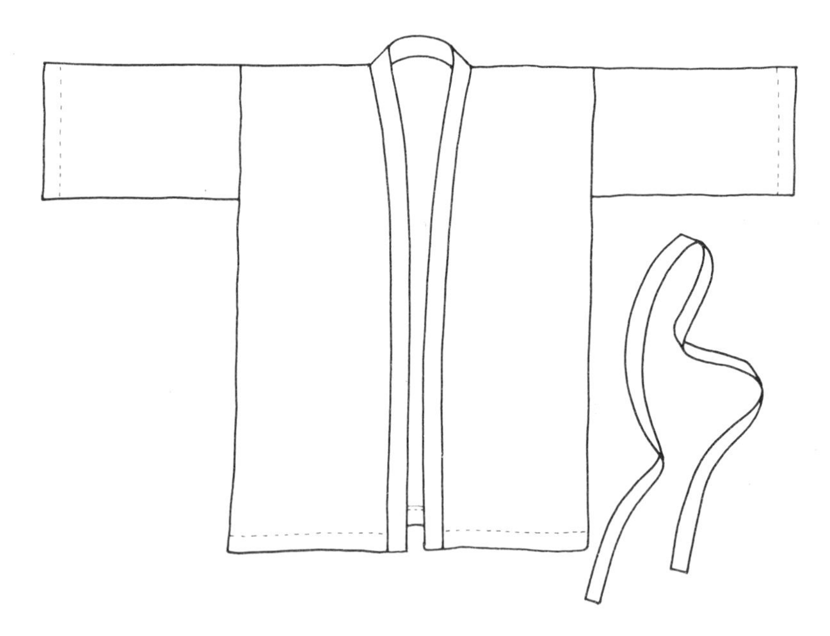

Instructions
Kimono

Material required: short kimono, 190 × 140 cm or 250 × 90 cm; long kimono, 285 × 140 cm or 340 × 90 cm.
Seam allowance: 2 cm all round.

Cut out. Press the band double and attach around the front edge and neck from hem to hem. Attach the sleeves between the marks shown on the pattern; then sew the side and sleeve seams in one go. Turn up the hem and cuffs. Sew and turn the sash.

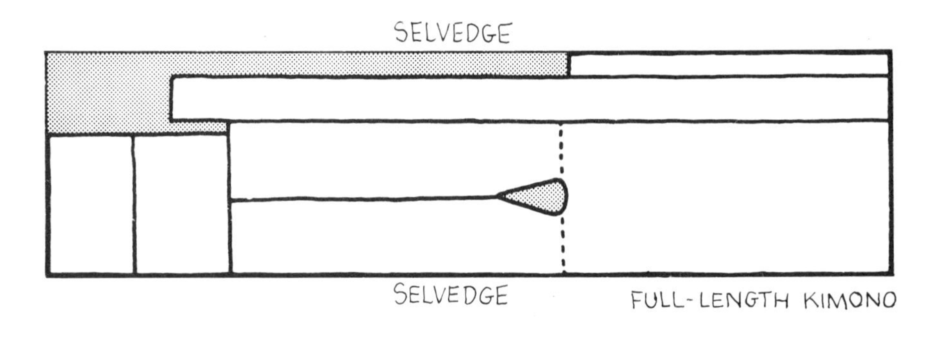

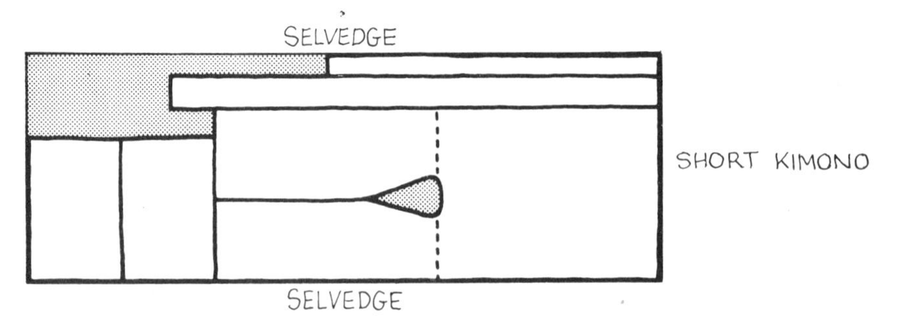

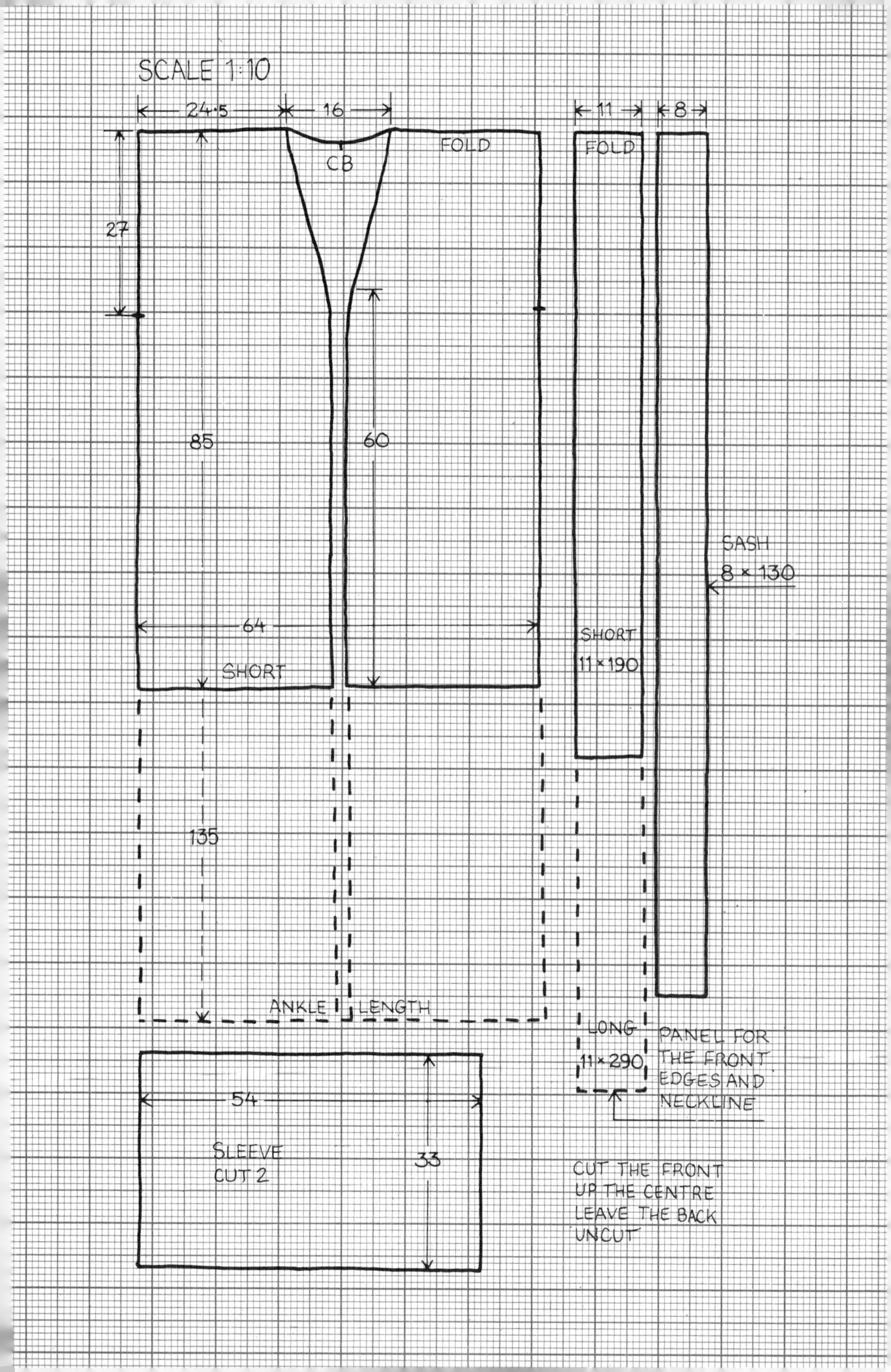
SCALE 1:10
24·5
16
27
FOLD
CB
85
60
64
SHORT
135
ANKLE LENGTH
11
8
FOLD
SASH
8 × 130
SHORT
11 × 190
LONG
11 × 290
PANEL FOR THE FRONT EDGES AND NECKLINE
54
33
SLEEVE
CUT 2
CUT THE FRONT UP THE CENTRE
LEAVE THE BACK UNCUT

African dress

The African dress is basically very similar to the Roman tunic: a sack with holes for the head and arms. With wide pointed sleeves sewn on at right angles, it is worn by Arab women in Israel and by women in West Africa, where the garment is called an 'apollo'. The dress can be full-length or it can be shorter and worn over a wrap-round skirt (see p. 162).

A simpler version of the dress than the one shown here is made from a straight length of cloth, considerably wider than the shoulders, folded double, with a head hole and the sides left open down to the hips for armholes. In this way a softly falling sleeve is formed.

This beautiful garment is simple to make, but has a strong impact, and can be made from any weight or quality of cloth. If plain material is used, it can be decorated with braids of various colours and widths.

Instructions African dress

Material required: 310 × 90 cm.
Seam allowance: 2 cm all round.

Sew the shoulder seams. Bind the neck hole with bias binding (see p. 15). Sew the shoulder seam of the sleeves right sides together and attach them to the body. Then sew round the side seam from the point of the sleeve to the hem of the dress in one go, preferably using a French seam (see p. 14). Turn up the hem, and hem the sleeves.

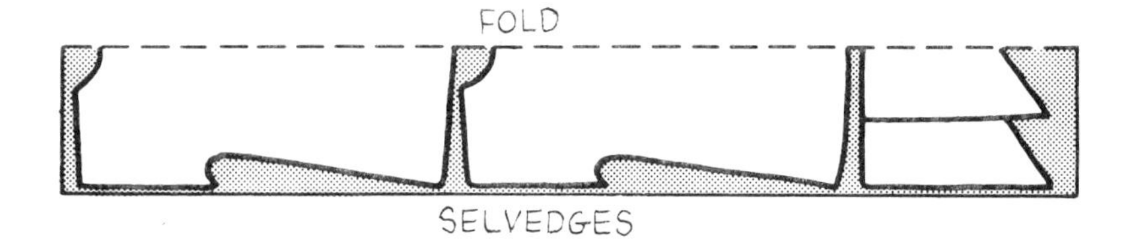

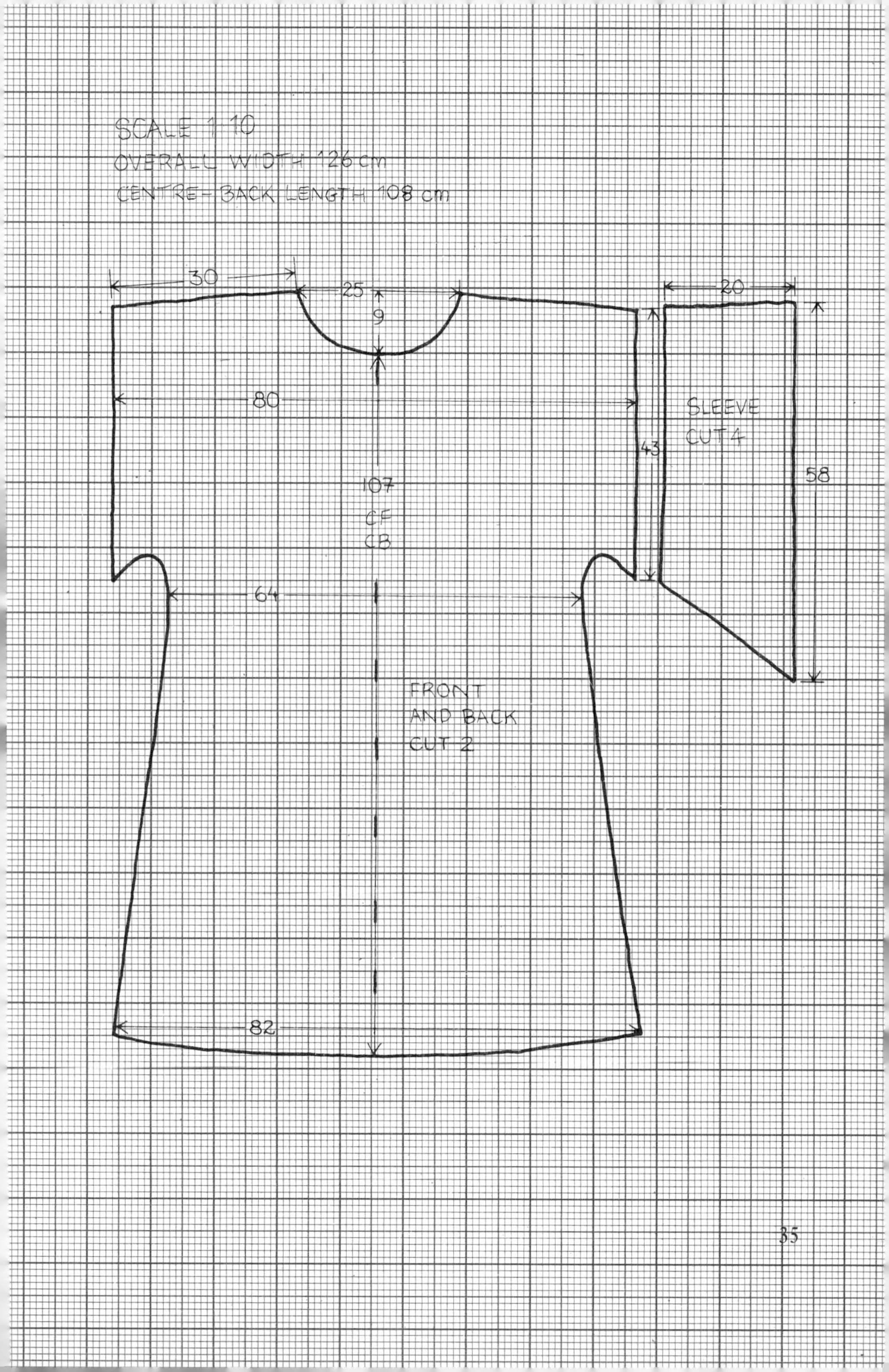
SCALE 1:10
OVERALL WIDTH 126 cm
CENTRE-BACK LENGTH 108 cm
30
25
9
80
43
107
CF
CB
64
FRONT
AND BACK
CUT 2
82
20
SLEEVE
CUT 4
58

Heavy-duty apron

The heavy-duty apron used to be made from tanned calf or cowhide. Unlike the ordinary apron, which has an equally long history, it was never taken up by the middle classes, but was worn for practical protection by working men and tradesmen. Plasterers wore a short version in chamois leather, shoemakers a slightly longer one, while men delivering coal, iron, ice and oil wore one which covered the whole front of the body to the knee or below. In one of the regions of Sweden it was known as a 'skimpy' and would be worn to church when new.

It can of course be made in the traditional leather, but it is cheaper in oilcloth, sailcloth or denim. It can have as many pockets as needed, and may be worn by either sex.

Instructions
Heavy-duty apron

Material required: 180 × 90 cm.
Seam allowance: 2 cm at top and sides, 3 cm at the hem.

Cut out; if possible, cut the neck facing with the bottom edge on the selvedge so that it will not need to be hemmed. Sew and turn the belt and neck strap. Hem by machine round the sides. Hem under bottom edge of neck facing. Lay the neck facing on the apron right sides together, sew and turn. Measure the length of the neck strap and fix both ends behind the apron at the neck points. Reinforce the top of the apron with lines of stitching between the two neck points. Attach both belt pieces securely where marked on the pattern. Make a button-hole on the right-hand side large enough to thread the belt through before tying it in front. Turn up the hem.

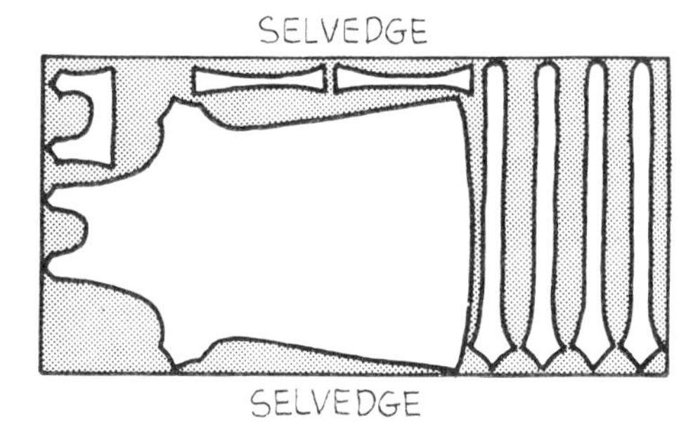

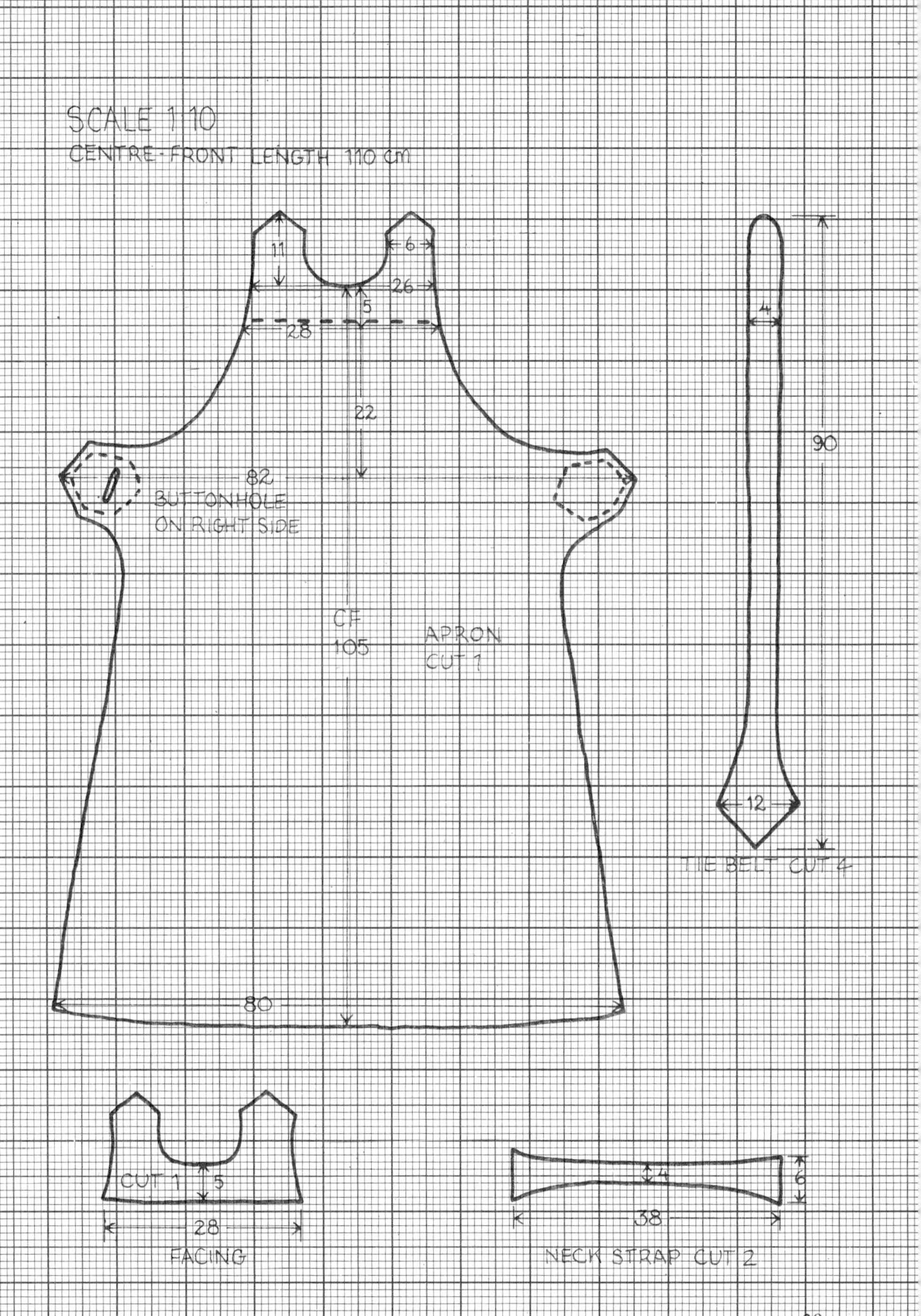

SCALE 1 10
CENTRE-FRONT LENGTH 110 cm
11
6
26
5
28
22
82
BUTTONHOLE
ON RIGHT SIDE
CF
105
APRON
CUT 1
80
4
90
12
TIE BELT CUT 4
CUT 1
5
28
FACING
4
6
38
NECK STRAP CUT 2

Dungarees

Dungarees developed spontaneously after the turn of the century out of two garments: the standard blue working trousers and the lumber-jacket. Their special character is created by the bib and braces, which replaced the jacket for practical reasons. Under the bib, carpenters wore a smock or shirt or whatever they liked.

The fit and design of workmen's trousers also improved around this time. Carpenters' dungarees, for instance, were fitted with a loop on the hip for carrying a hammer, then a ruler pocket on the leg and a breast pocket with a place for a carpenter's pencil, and other handy features.

The style is the same for men and women, and the aim of the garment is general practicality and freedom of movement. Dungarees can serve as a substitute for trousers; and although they are generously cut one can be sure they will stay up.

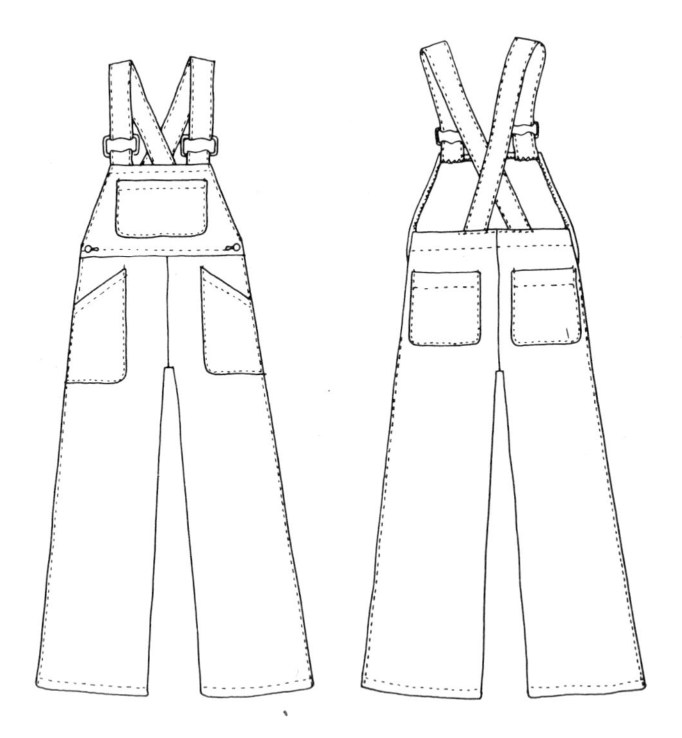

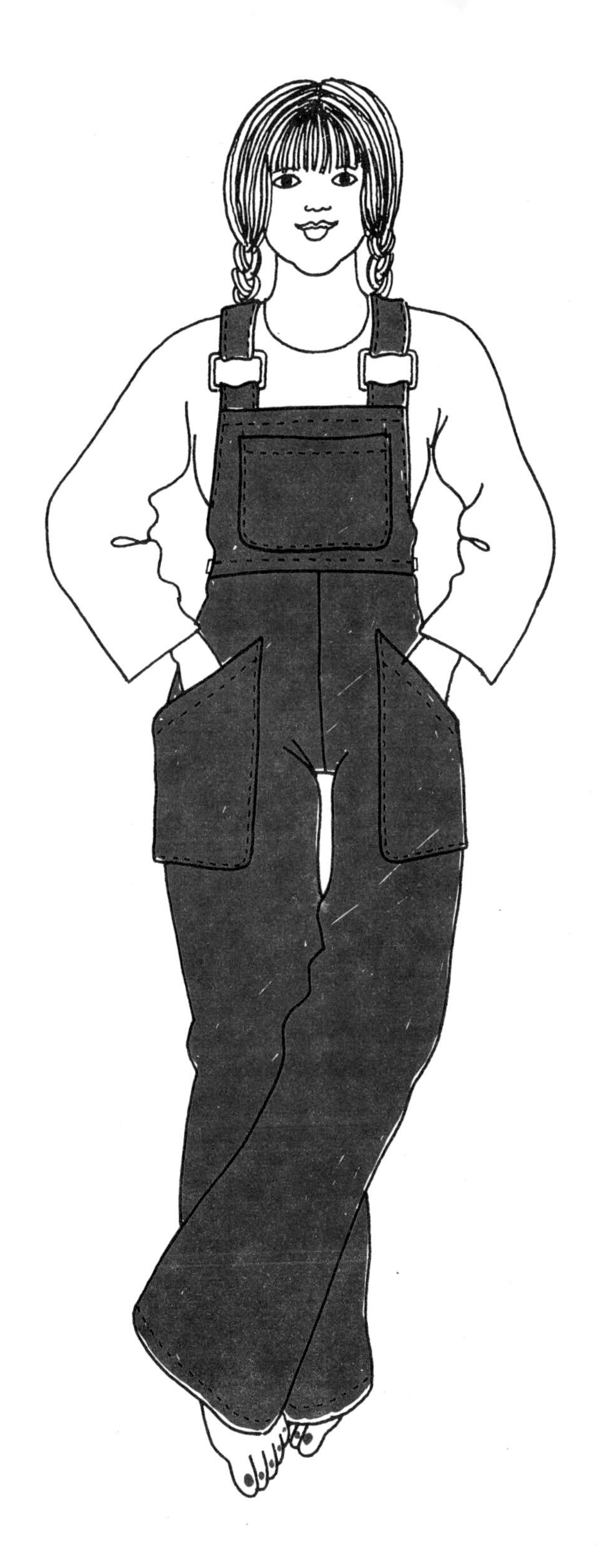

Instructions
Dungarees

Material required: 230 × 140 cm; two large metal rings; two buttons; zip fastener if desired.
Seam allowance: 2 cm all round.

Sew and turn the braces and loops. Top-stitch. Turn under the edges of the pockets and stitch them close to the fold, then sew them on where marked. Hem the top and sides of the bib.

Sew the outside seams of the trousers with a fell seam (see p. 15), and top-stitch 1 cm from the seam. Sew up to the side openings as marked on the pattern. Hem the openings with a narrow turning front and back. Sew the inside leg seams and press. Turn one leg inside out and push the other leg into it with the inside seams meeting. Sew the crotch seam. If you want a zip fastening in front, sew only up to the fly markings. Press the seam allowance in and tack the zip in position. Stitch from the right side.

Attach the bib to the trousers, right sides together, with the bib centred on the front seam of the trousers. Sew 5 cm down from the edge. Turn the bib up, fold under 1 cm of the trouser top seam allowance, and sew 3·5 cm from the first seam.

Tack the facing to the back of the trousers right sides together, stitch, turn to the inside and fold, and stitch 3·5 cm from the edge. Hem the trousers to the length required.

Sew the braces firmly on either side of the back seam. Fold the two loops in half lengthwise, thread a metal ring on each and sew them securely to the top of the bib, one at each side. Cross the braces over at the back, thread the free ends through the metal rings, make sure that they are the right length and sew securely.

On both side openings attach a button on the back and make the corresponding buttonhole in the front.

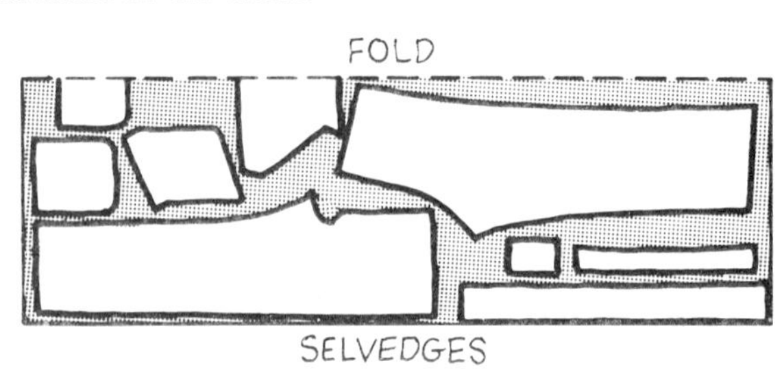

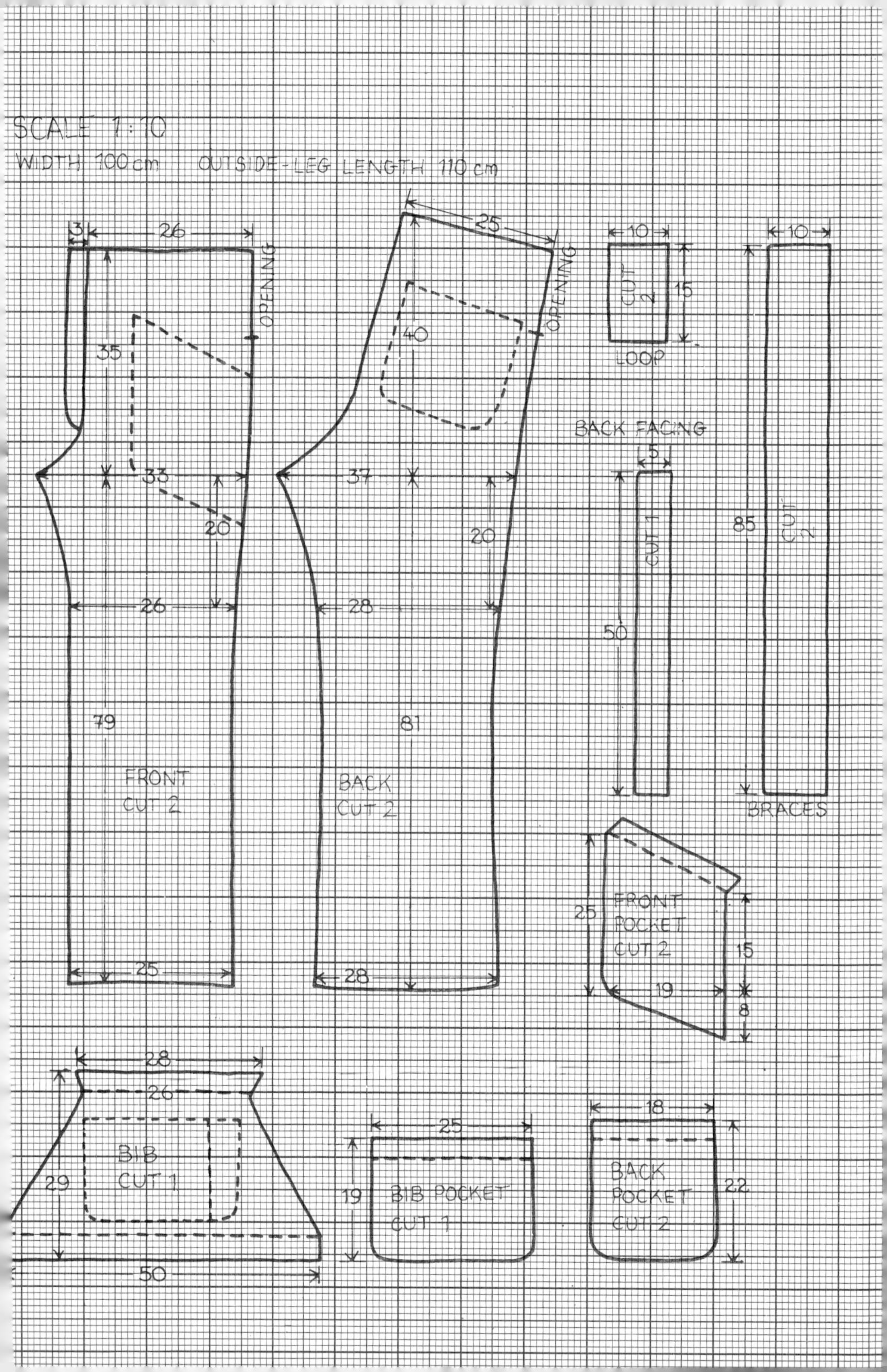
SCALE 1:10
WIDTH 100 cm OUTSIDE-LEG LENGTH 110 cm
3
26
OPENING
35
33
20
26
79
FRONT
CUT 2
25
25
OPENING
40
37
20
28
81
BACK
CUT 2
28
10
CUT 2
15
LOOP
BACK FACING
5
CUT 1
50
10
85
CUT 2
BRACES
25
FRONT
POCKET
CUT 2
15
19
8
28
26
BIB
CUT 1
29
50
25
19
BIB POCKET
CUT 1
18
BACK
POCKET
CUT 2
22

Child's trousers

Instructions

Material required: 165 × 90 cm; elastic for the waist.
Seam allowance: 1·5 cm on the side and crotch seams, 3 cm at the waist, 5 cm at the bottom of the legs.

Sew the outside leg seams and press open. Sew the inside leg seams and after that the crotch seam as in the dungarees (p. 42). Fold down 3 cm from the top to make a casing for the elastic. Insert elastic. Hem the legs.

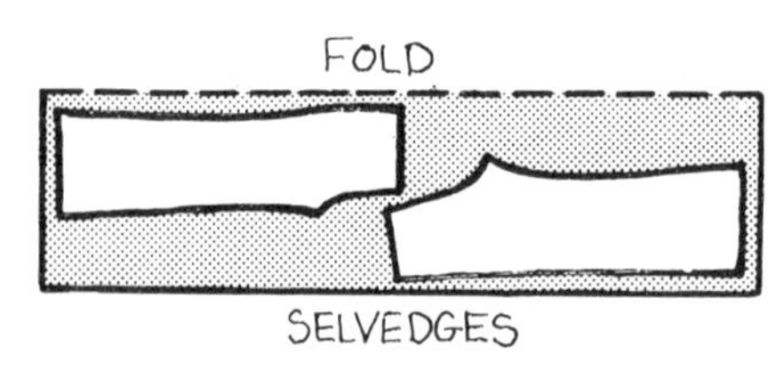

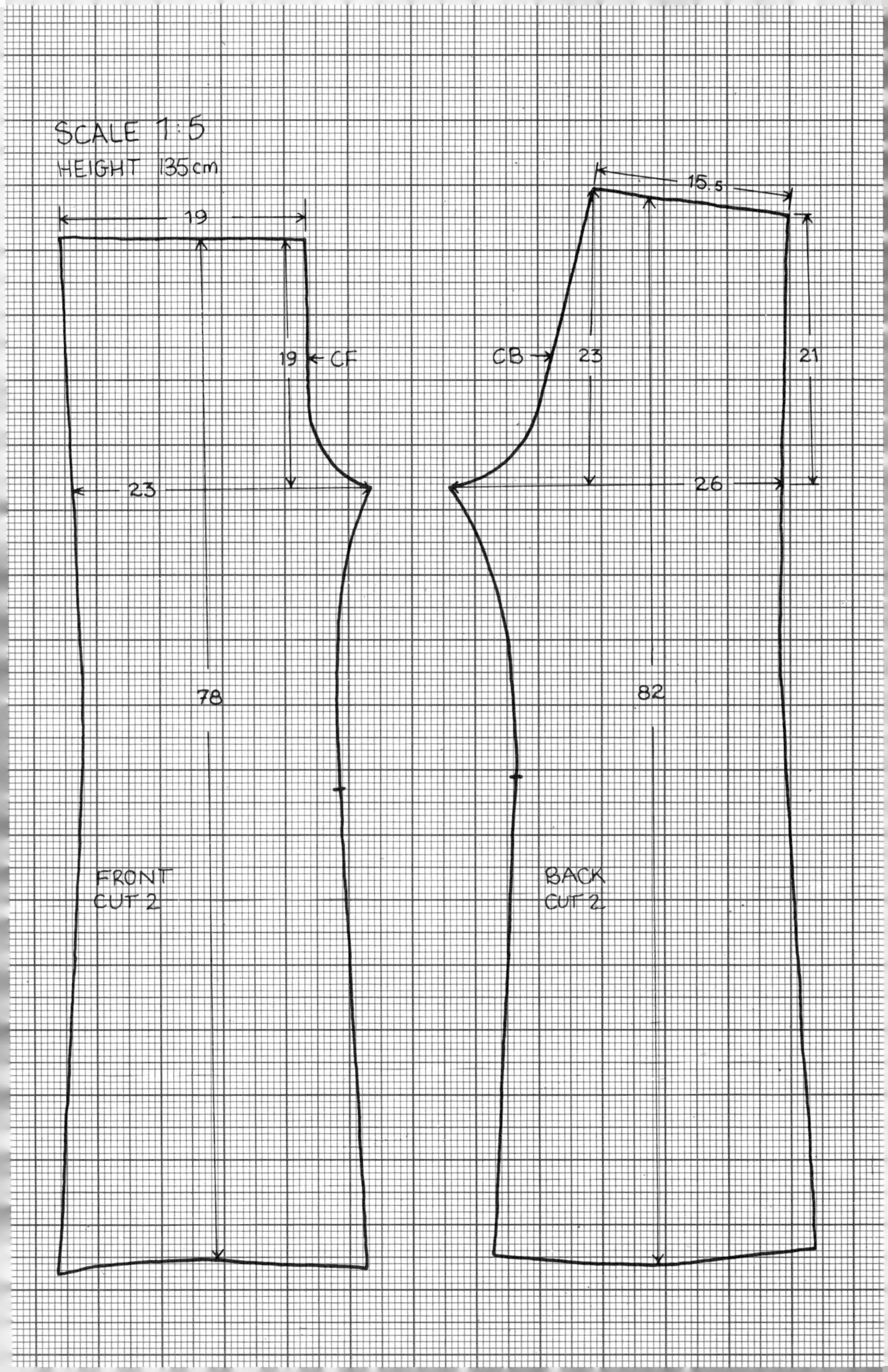
SCALE 1:5
HEIGHT 135cm
19
19
CF
23
78
FRONT
CUT 2
15.5
CB
23
21
26
82
BACK
CUT 2

Moccasins

Moccasins are, of course, the footwear of the American Indians. They are made from one or more pieces of skin, which are tied round the foot and gathered into a seam at the back of the heel.

Tough but not hard skin should be used; moccasins of dyed sheepskin with the fleece inside are warm as well as beautiful.

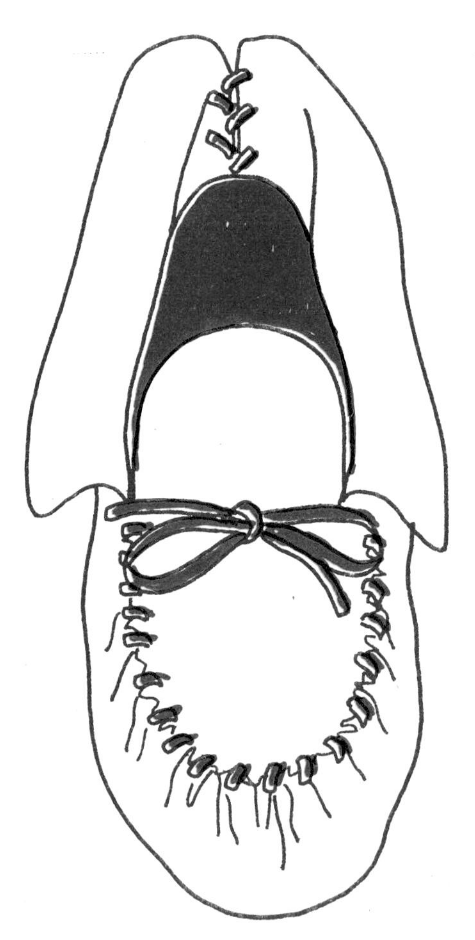

Instructions
Moccasins

Material required: size 12 (child's), 60 × 25 cm; size 5, 65 × 35 cm.

Cut out the skin *without* making any seam allowance. If you want a collar, cut around the outer line; if not, round the inner line. Be very precise about marking the holes so that there are the same number in top and bottom pieces. Make the holes with a leather punch. Lace together with thongs.

SCALE 1:5
SIZES 5 AND 12 (CHILD'S)

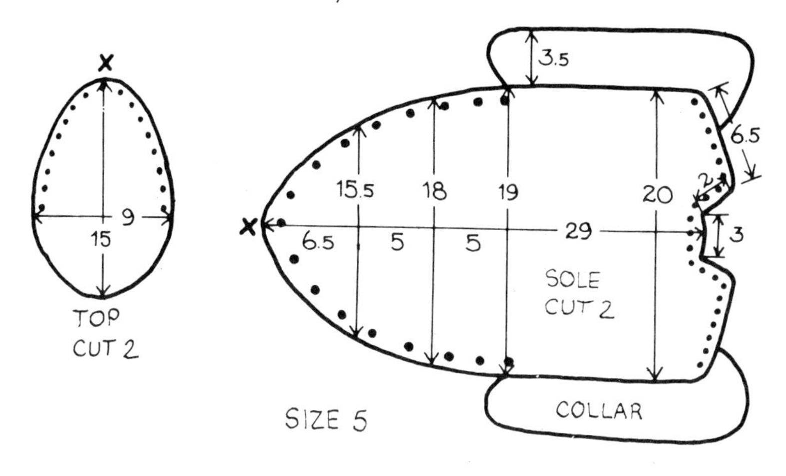

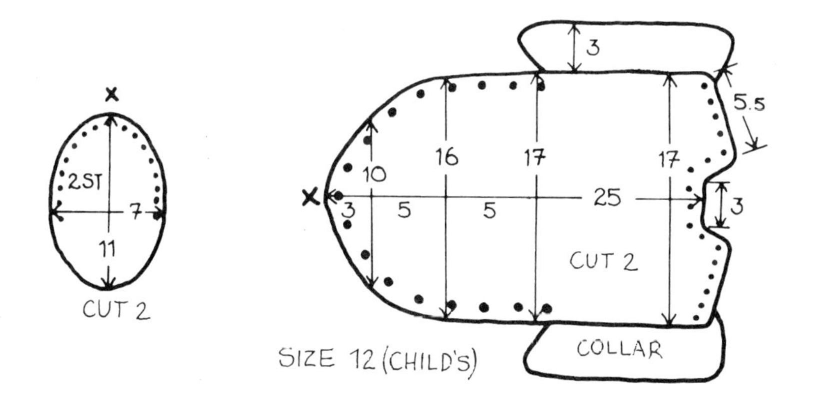

Lapp coat

The Lapps wear a warm coat drawn on over the head. In the old days the drop shoulders used to be a feature of the garment, but nowadays it is often cut in the same way as a modern jacket. The style varies greatly in different parts of the country. The northern Lapps decorate it with several rows of coloured braid; in southern regions the coat is longer; in Jokkmokk it has become plainer and has only one band of colour on the front. These coats are worn only by men. The women have a longer dress which resembles the coat but is often collarless.

Everyday coats are made of grey or yellowish-green homespun cloth, while the Sunday coat is of blue cloth. The coloured bands are also of cloth, except in the more northerly parts, where they can be done with woven edging braid. There are also coats made of tanned skin which are very costly.

The coat can be made of any wool or cloth of medium weight with enough body to carry the bias binding and braid. For maximum decorative effect you can join several narrow braids into one wide one of different colours and patterns.

Tie at the neck
A variation of the Lapp coat can be made without braid, but with a breast pocket and tie belt

Instructions
Lapp coat

Material required (adult): 310 × 90 cm; bias binding, 320 cm; braid (5 cm wide if possible), 370 cm.
Material required (child): 185 × 90 cm; bias binding, 245 cm; braid, 265 cm.
Seam allowance: 1 cm round the neck and the bottom edge of the collar, nothing on the top edge of the collar, 1·5 cm round the main pieces, 5 cm for the hem.

Use braid in one colour and bias binding for edging in a contrasting colour to give the best decorative effect.

Pin the collar pieces together right sides outwards. Tack braid to the top edge of the collar, stretching it round the curve. Sew 5 mm from the top edge of the collar and at the bottom edge of the braid. Right side uppermost, make several rows of stitching along the collar at 7 mm intervals for decoration.

Unfold one edge of the bias binding and pin to the long edges of the two yoke pieces, right sides together. Sew 1·5 cm in from the edge. Leave it folded out. Sew the yoke to the front and back pieces right sides together, sewing along the line of stitching attaching the bias binding. Press so that the seams open on the inside, and the bias binding lies open upwards on the yoke. Turn the bias binding down over the seam and stitch.

Sew the centre-back seam and, as on the yoke, include in the seam a length of bias binding which runs 20 cm down from the neck of the

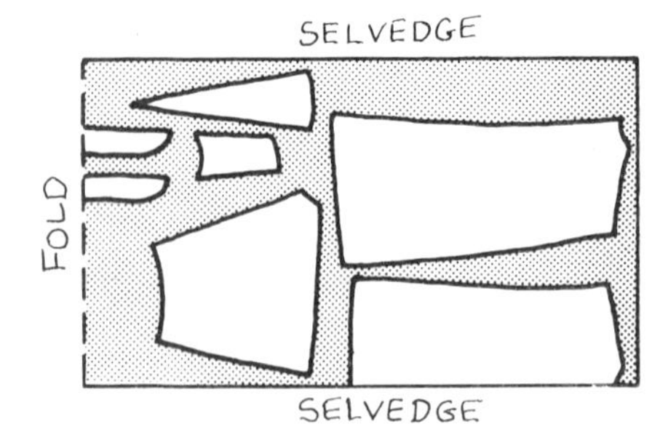

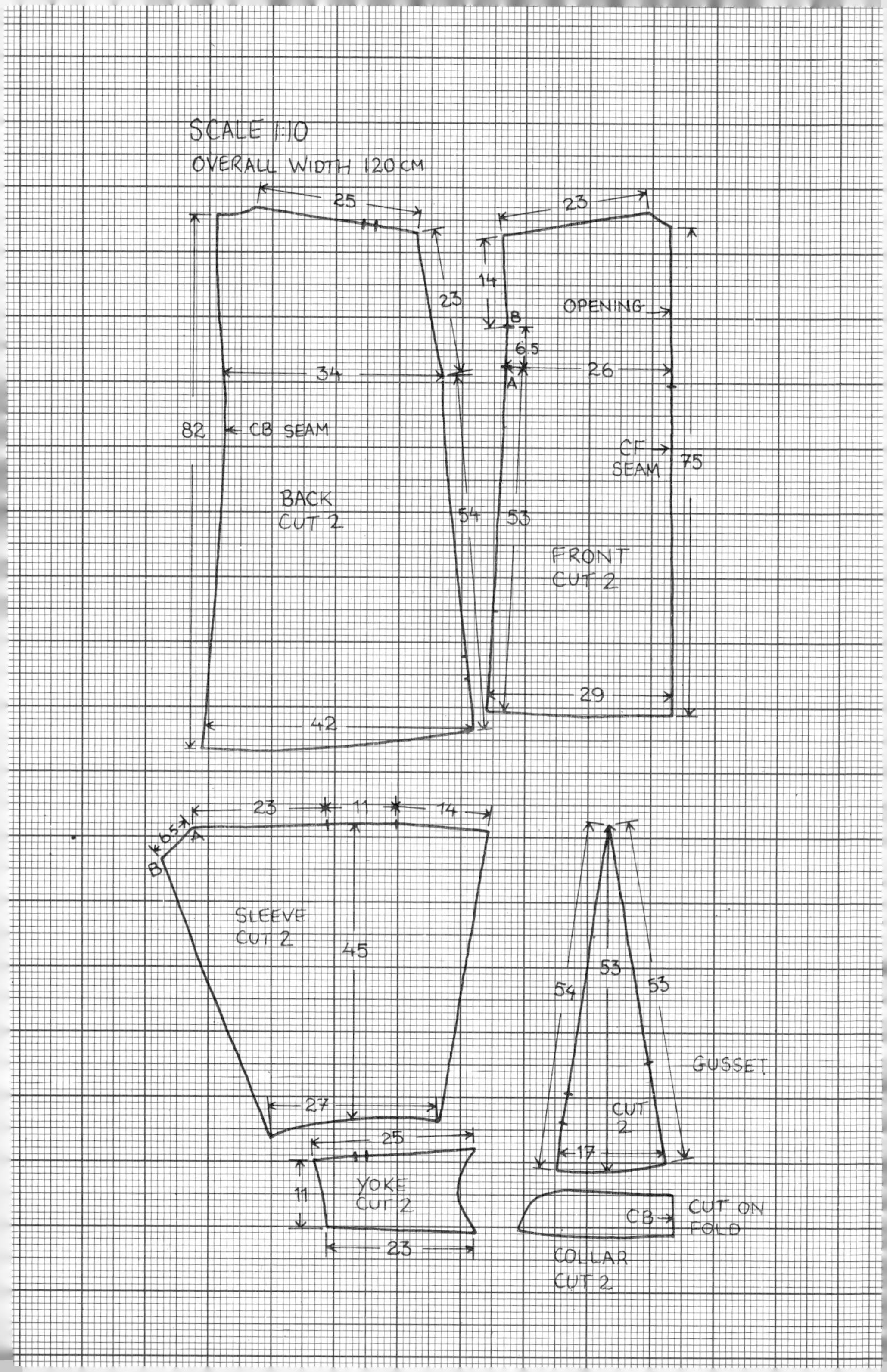
SCALE 1:10
OVERALL WIDTH 120 CM
25
23
82
CB SEAM
34
BACK
CUT 2
54
42
23
14
B
6.5
A
OPENING
26
CF
SEAM
75
53
FRONT
CUT 2
29
B
6.5
A
23
11
14
SLEEVE
CUT 2
45
27
25
11
YOKE
CUT 2
23
54
53
53
GUSSET
CUT
2
17
CB
CUT ON
FOLD
COLLAR
CUT 2

child's size and 30 cm in the adult's. Press the bias binding to one side, and stitch down. Finish the seam.

On the right side sew braid down both sides of the front opening, letting it go 3 cm below the bottom of the opening. Turn under the ends of the braid and sew round its outer edge. Sew the front seam up to the opening marks. Press open and finish the seam. Trim the seam allowance on the front opening to 7 mm.

Pin the collar to the body wrong sides together so that the seam opens towards the right side. Tack bias binding on the right side round the neckline, then sew collar and bias binding on in one go. Press the binding up and pin it to the collar so that it covers the seam. Stitch it near the edge. Then bind the top edge of the collar and the front opening with bias binding.

Sew the gussets into the side seams. Press and finish the seams.

Sew the sleeve seams, press and finish. At the cuff, turn up 5 mm towards the right side. Sew braid over the turning. Pin in the sleeves according to the A and B markings in the diagram. Note that the sleeve seam does *not* marry up with the side seam (see drawing). Finish. Strengthen the underarm by sewing a row of stitching from the right side.

Hem the garment. Sew braid on the right side over the hem. Press. Sew a decorative hook and eye on the neck opening.

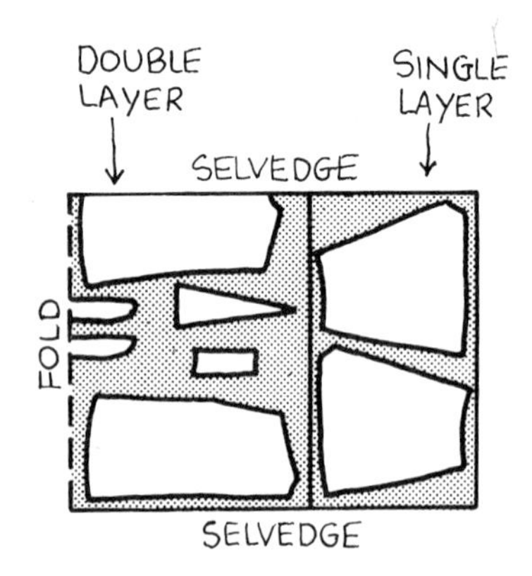

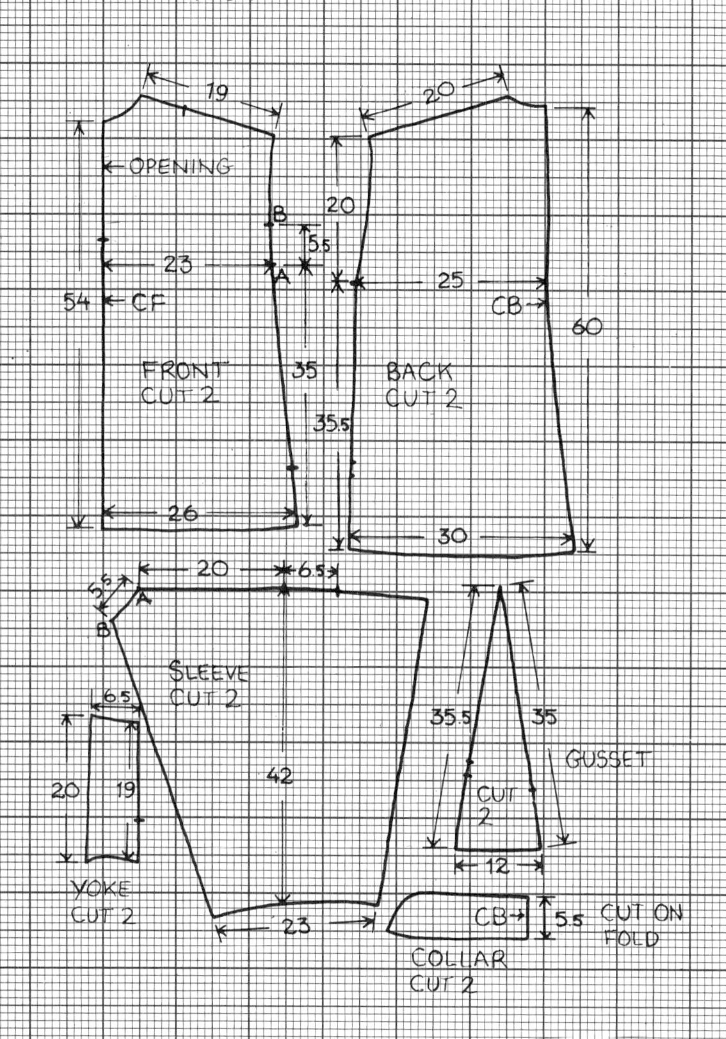

Lapp coat child's size

Parka

As far as we know, parka is the Canadian name for the Eskimo anorak. There are Eskimos along the whole of the north coast of Canada, and no doubt there are local variations in the cut of the garment. But basically the parka is a very roomy skin coat drawn on over the head. It is made of seal or deerskin and is fitted with a warm hood, exactly like the anorak.

This garment became generally known through the Korean war in the early 1950s, when the Americans wore a lined cotton jacket with big pockets and a fur-lined hood, and called it a parka.

This modern version opens at the front with buttons or a zip.

Without
buttons,
fur
trimmings

Instructions
Parka

Material required (adult): 225 × 140 cm; buttons or a zip, cord and two eyelets.
Material required (child): 140 × 140 cm; buttons or a zip, cord and two eyelets.
Seam allowance: 1·5 cm round all pieces, 5 cm at the cuffs and hem.

The garment can be made from any coat-weight material, preferably waterproof. Thin materials like wind poplin should be sewn with fell seams (see p. 15). For other fabrics, ordinary seams will do.

Sew the shoulders with fell seams. Tack the sleeves to the body and sew, using fell seams. Sew the sleeve and side seams in one go. Hem the tops of the pockets. Press in the seam allowances on the pockets and the belt casing. Hem the ends of the casing. Attach the pockets and the waist casing as marked on the pattern.

Using a fell seam, sew the two side pieces of the hood together at the top, and sew on the back piece. If the hood is not going to be lined, it is better to use a French seam. Put a small piece of interfacing on the inside of the hood to strengthen the points at the base of the hood where the eyelets are to be fitted. Hammer the eyelets in. Fold in the front turning of the hood, and sew close to the front edge from the right side. Pull a cord through the eyelets and place it under this turning. Then sew round the front of the hood again, 2 cm away from the front edge, thus enclosing the drawstring in the hem.

Tack the hood to the garment, right sides together, centre backs

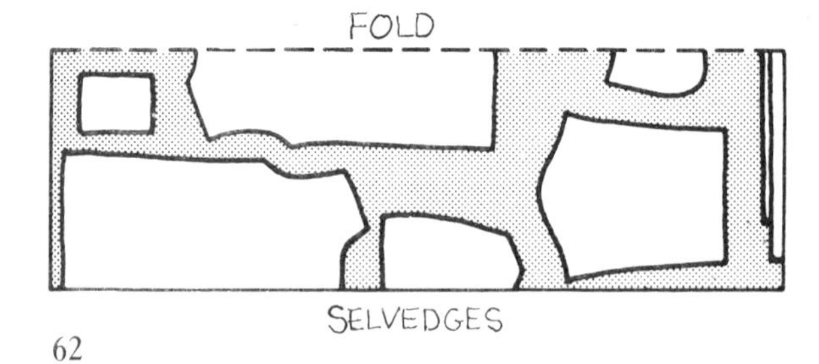

SCALE 1:10

OVERALL WIDTH 118 cm LENGTH AT CENTRE BACK 92 cm

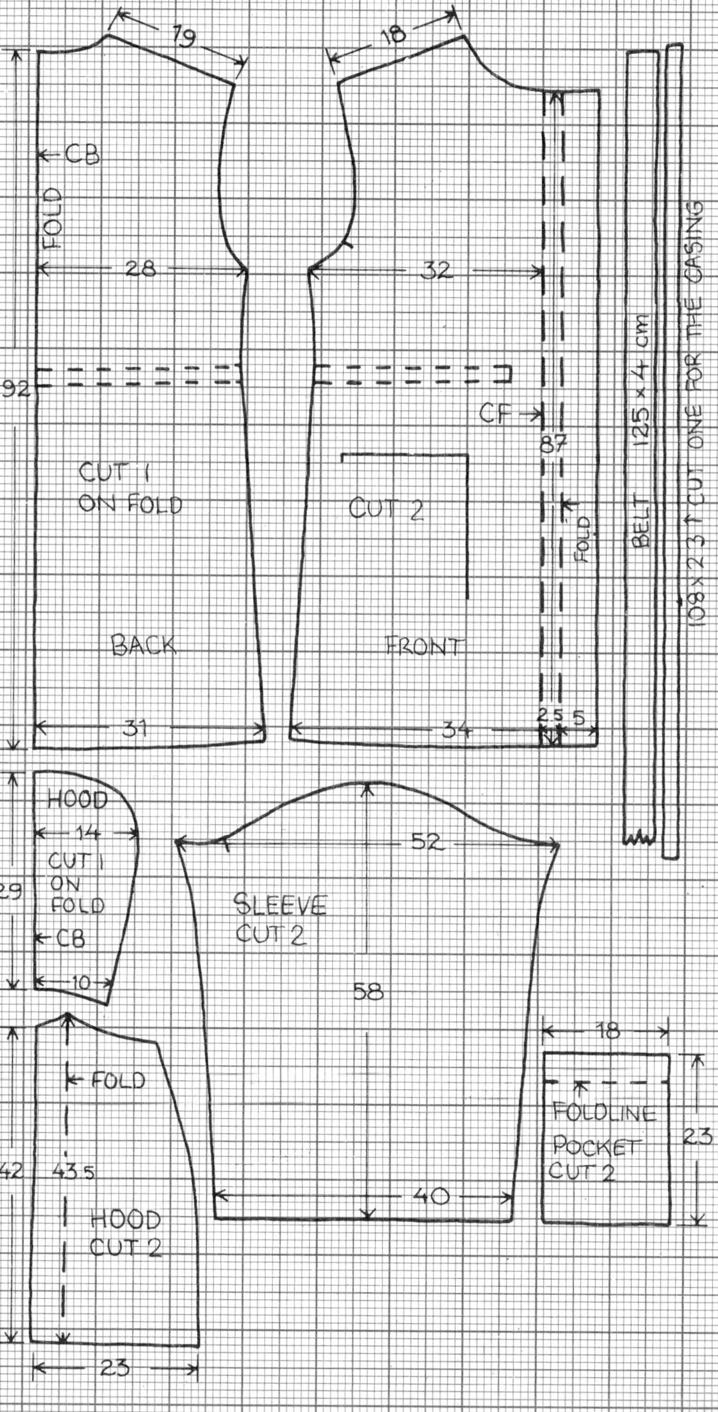

matching. Fold back the front facings of the jacket on the right side,* and sew right round the neckline. Turn the front facings to the inside and press. If the coat is unlined, binding the neck seam with a piece of bias binding will make it more comfortable.

Machine hem the cuffs and bottom. Sew the tie belt, turn it right side out, press and top-stitch. Pull it through the casing at the waist. Mark and sew buttonholes and buttons, or sew in the zip following the instructions on the packet. Press.

To line the body of these parkas follow the same pattern using fake fur, cotton flannel, quilted or other material. Attach fur round the hood.

* If the parka is to be fastened with a zip, fold the facings on the centre-front line, not the fold line.

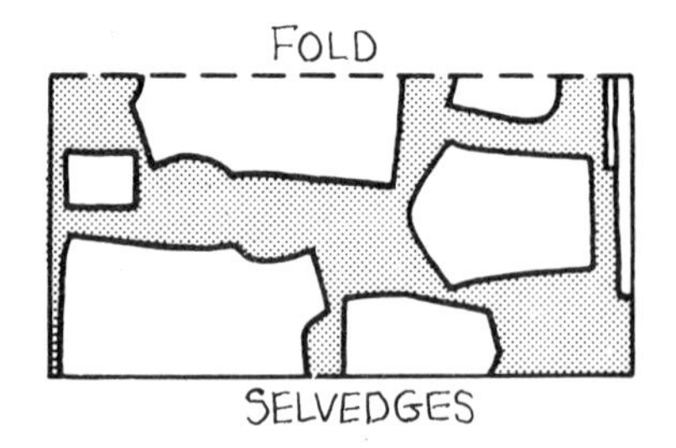

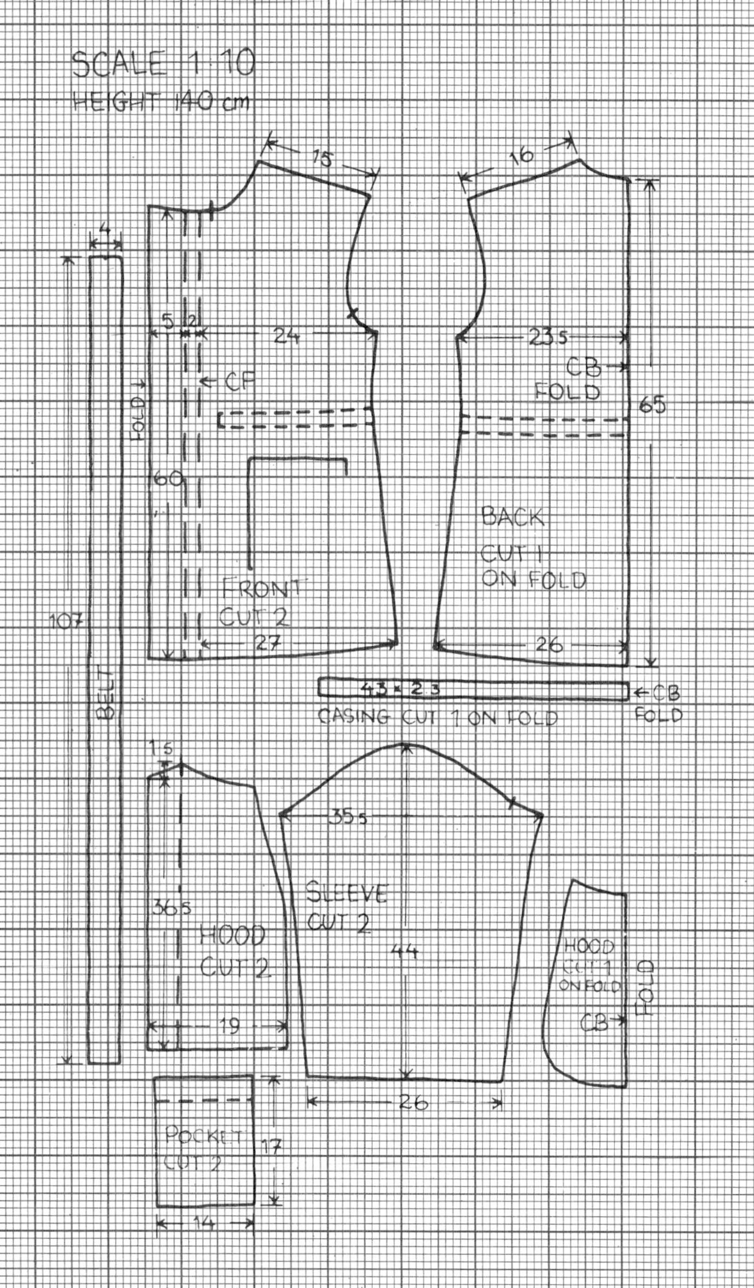

Parka child's size

Camisole top

This was an item of underwear worn by middle-class ladies at the turn of the century, and also in a simpler version by country women. First known as a corset cover and later as an underblouse, it almost always buttoned in front.

Underwear in those days – from Paris, made in fine lawn, or home-produced in coarser cottons – was so beautifully and elaborately decorated that it is a rich source of ideas for us today, and is often worn nowadays for show.

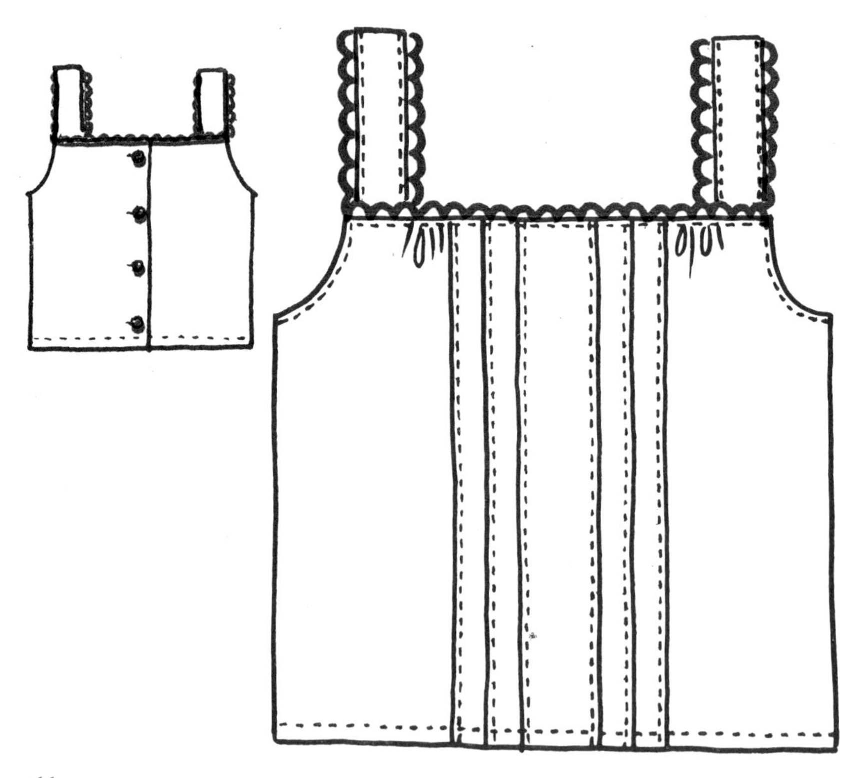

Instructions
Camisole top

Material required: 95 × 90 cm; 260 cm rick-rack braid; four buttons.
Seam allowance: 1 cm around all pieces.

Mark the tucks on the front pieces and sew them on the right side of the fabric. Press them towards the sides.

Run a double gathering thread on each side of the tucks to the armholes, as shown on the pattern. Gather so that the width of the front matches that of the facing. Sew the side seams of the bodice and of the facing. Finish the seams and press open. Hem the bottom of the yoke facing. Hem the back facing.

Fold the shoulder straps, wrong sides together, sew, turn right side out and press. Tack the braid to the underside of the shoulder straps. Top-stitch from the right side.

Lay the braid along the top edge of the bodice, front and back, from armhole to armhole, on the right side of the fabric. Attach with a line of stitching along the centre of the braid, about 1 cm from the edge of the bodice pieces.

Lay the shoulder straps running vertically down the front pieces from the top edge near the armholes to the bottom, right sides together and attach firmly. Turn the centre-back facings to the outside. Now place the yoke facing on the bodice on top of the straps and the braid, right sides together, top edges matching. Baste firmly. Sew from the wrong side along the line of stitching you used to attach the braid. Turn the facing to the inside and press. Top-stitch from the right side close to the edge.

Hem the bodice. Mark and sew four buttonholes in the back. Attach the buttons. Measure the correct length for the shoulder straps. Sew them to the back by hand. Press.

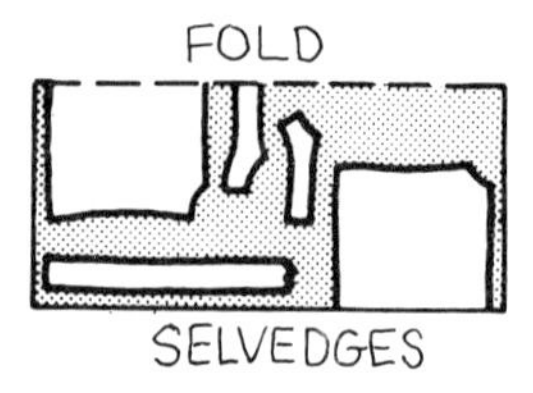

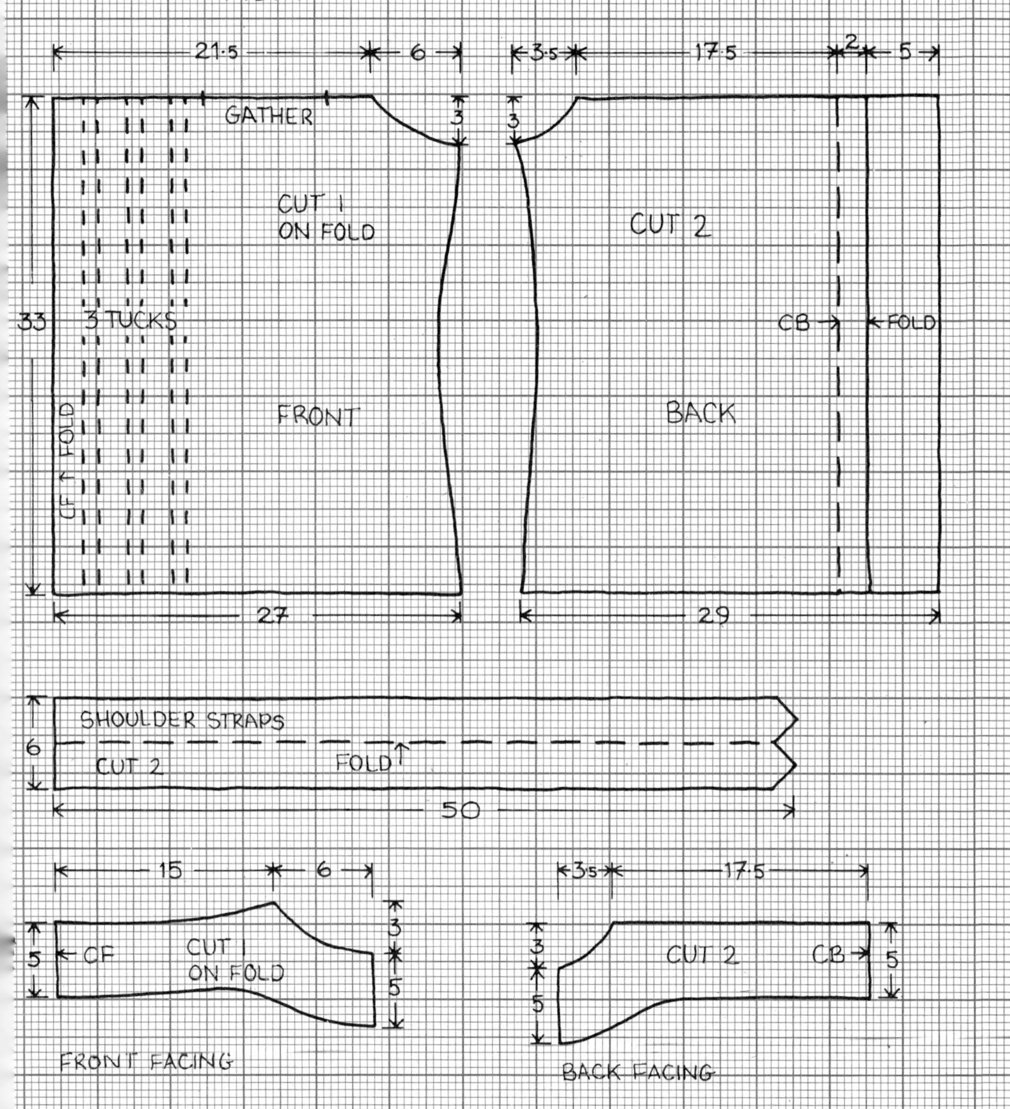
SCALE 1:5
OVERALL WIDTH 92 cm
21·5
6
3.5
17·5
2
5
GATHER
3
3
CUT 1
ON FOLD
CUT 2
33
3 TUCKS
CB
FOLD
CF ↑ FOLD
FRONT
BACK
27
29
SHOULDER STRAPS
6
CUT 2
FOLD
50
15
6
3·5
17·5
5
CF
CUT 1
ON FOLD
3
5
3
5
CUT 2
CB
5
FRONT FACING
BACK FACING

Djellaba

Long, roomy overdress of the North African Arabs, made from wool, with long arms and a hood. Unlike the coat-like burnous, it is pulled on over the head.

City-dwellers normally wear a dark blue djellaba with a red border; otherwise the colours range from grey to brown in simple striped patterns which stand out beautifully in the rough wool.

The djellaba becomes a coat when it is buttoned and belted

Instructions
Djellaba

Material required: 225 × 135 cm; bias binding; braid.
Seam allowance: 1·5 cm around the edges of the sleeves, hood and gusset; 5 cm around the cuffs. Otherwise nothing.

Fold the cloth double and slash it for the sleeves and gussets, marking the dart below the gusset.

Sew the shoulder seams and the darts. Finish the seams and press open. Sew one side of the gusset to the sleeve as marked (see also p. 17). Sew the sleeve seam and the other side of the gusset. Finish the seams and press. Tack the sleeves to the body, right sides together, and sew. Finish the seams.

Fold the hood right side out and sew the seam along the crown. Press the seam open and sew a bias strip over it on the right side. Fold and hem the front edge. Make the tucks on the neck of the hood and pin it to the neckline of the garment, wrong sides together. Turn the selvedge (seam allowance) at the front opening to the inside. Unfold one edge of some bias binding and tack it, right side down, on the right side of the hood, along the neckline, leaving enough over at the ends to make a button loop or lacing. Sew securely through binding, hood and garment. Press the bias binding down over the seam. Top-stitch near the edge.

Sew the front seam between the markings and press open. Hem the sleeves and the bottom. Sew braid over the centre-front seam. Fasten the neck with ties or with a button and loop.

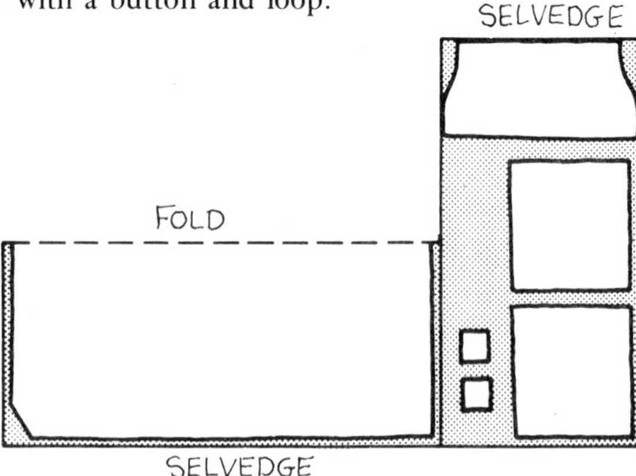

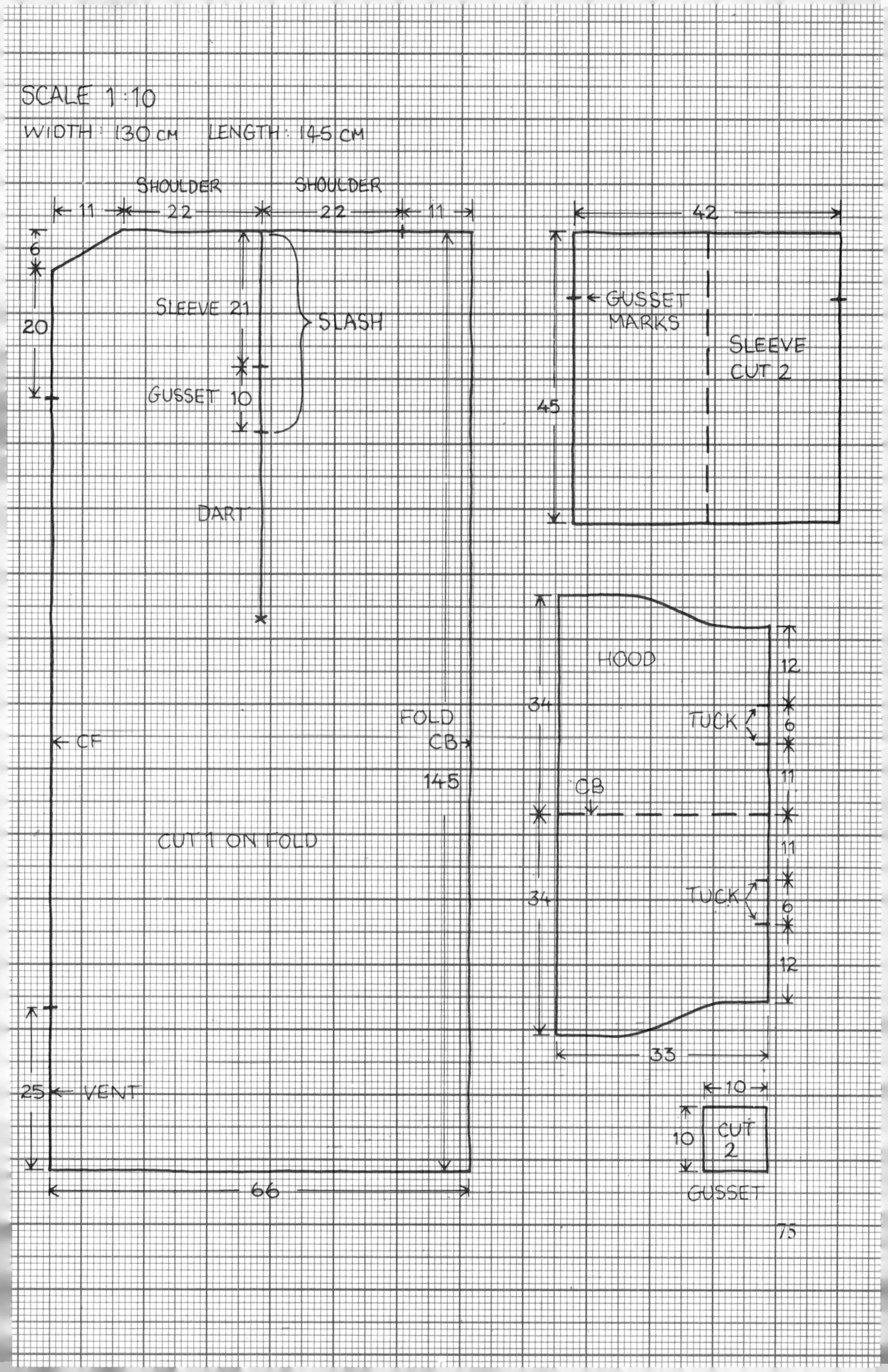

SCALE 1:10
WIDTH: 130 CM LENGTH: 145 CM
SHOULDER
SHOULDER
11
22
22
11
6
20
SLEEVE 21
GUSSET 10
SLASH
DART
FOLD
CB
145
CF
CUT 1 ON FOLD
25
VENT
66
42
GUSSET MARKS
SLEEVE CUT 2
45
HOOD
34
12
TUCK
6
11
CB
11
34
TUCK
6
12
33
10
10
CUT 2
GUSSET

Flared skirt

Short skirts and trousers for women only appeared after the First World War, although women's clothing had begun to allow greater freedom of movement from the turn of the century onwards. The corset was increasingly left off, and as women took up sporting and other outdoor activities – cycling, in particular – they wore skirts which gave them greater mobility.

This flared skirt was such a garment: it is made up of six pieces which are narrow at the top and widen towards the hem, allowing natural movement.

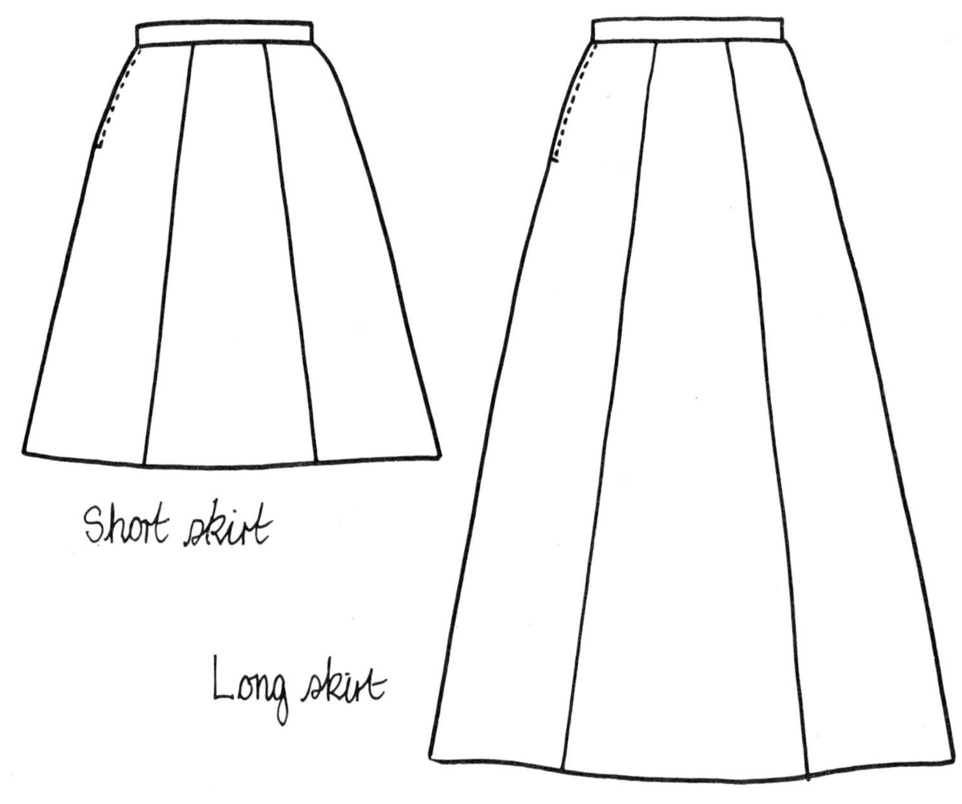

Three tucks at the hem
Three rows of frills made out of different materals

Trimming and frill
Short skirt with fell seams

Instructions
Flared skirt

Material required: short skirt, 140 × 190 cm; long skirt, 180 × 190 cm; long skirt with frill, 255 × 90 cm; 20 cm zip. Before making the pattern or buying the material be sure to check the length of skirt you want.
Seam allowance: 1 cm around the waist and waistband, 1·5 cm on all long seams, 4 cm at the hem.

Tack the panels together and try on. Make necessary adjustments for fitting and sew. Leave an opening at the left side for the zip. Press the side seams open; press the front seams towards the centre front, the back ones towards the centre back.

The waistband needs stiffening if thin or soft material is used. To do this sew a piece of petersham or other stiff fabric along one side. Fold the waistband in half lengthwise, right sides together and sew across the ends, sewing in a button loop at one end. Turn the waistband right side out and press. Tack the zip at the left side and sew. Sew one edge of the waistband to the top of the skirt, right sides together. (See that the button loop is at the front.) Turn it up and press the seam upwards. Turn under the seam allowance on the other edge of the waistband and sew on the inside by hand. Sew button to waistband. Hem the skirt and press.

Note: The long skirt with the frill is sewn as above but not hemmed at the bottom. For the frill, cut out three straight pieces 25 × 90 cm across the width of the cloth. Sew together the short sides of the frill. Make a small hem on the frill by machine. Sew two gathering threads along the top and gather evenly. Tack and then sew the frill to the skirt. Press.

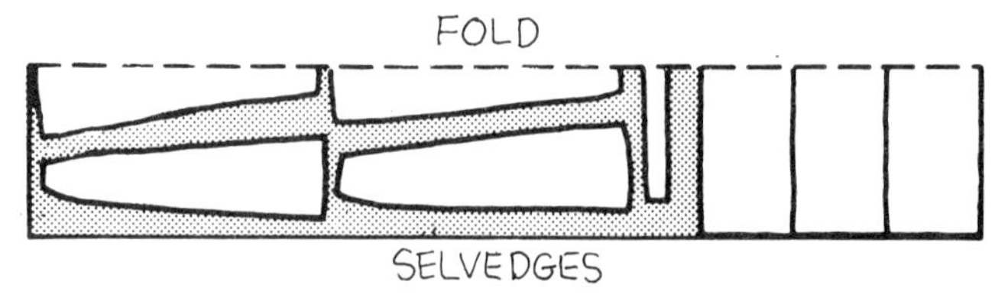

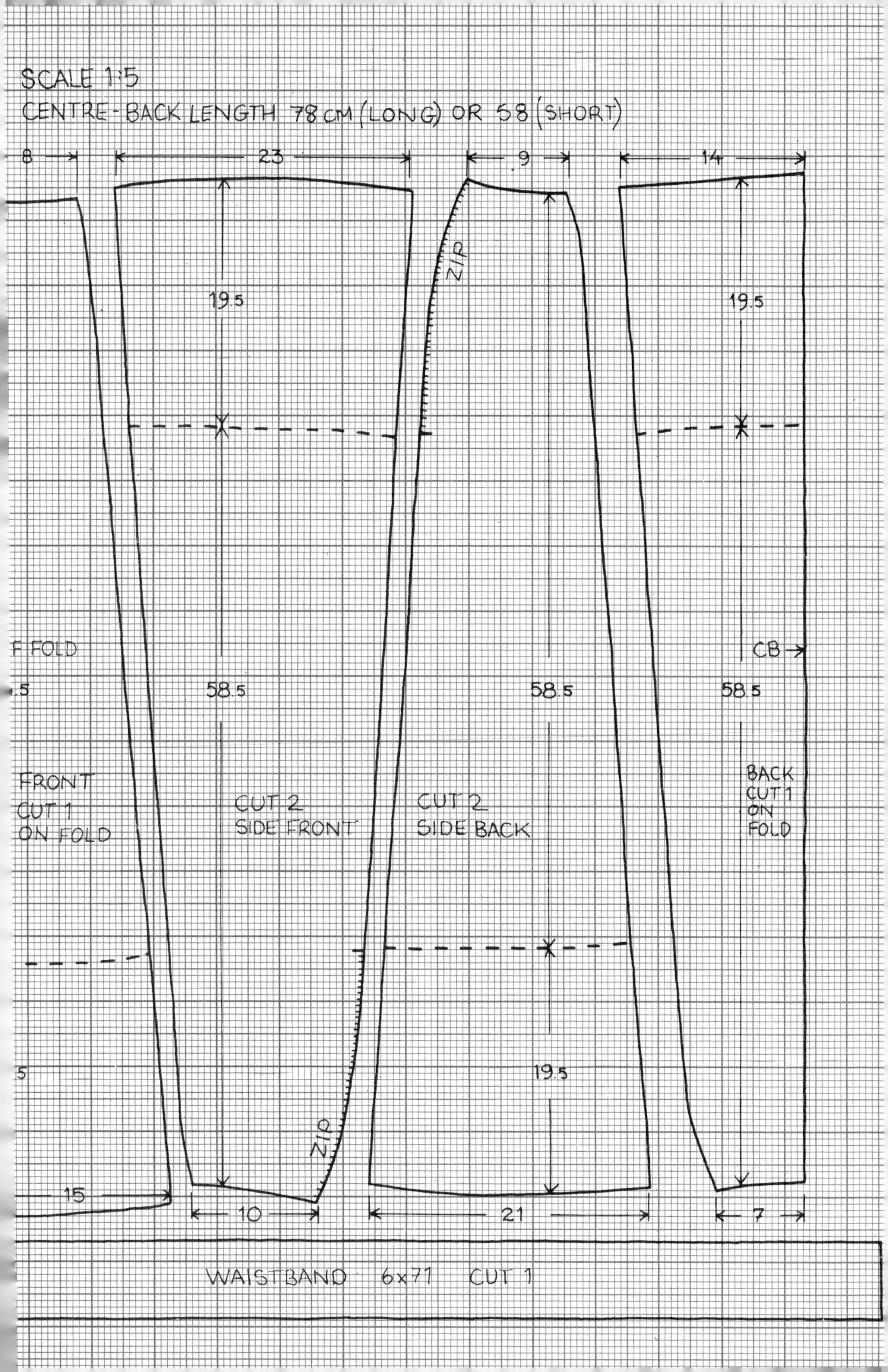

SCALE 1:5
CENTRE-BACK LENGTH 78 CM (LONG) OR 58 (SHORT)
8
23
9
14
19.5
19.5
ZIP
F FOLD
CB
.5
58.5
58.5
58.5
FRONT
CUT 1
ON FOLD
CUT 2
SIDE FRONT
CUT 2
SIDE BACK
BACK
CUT 1
ON
FOLD
5
19.5
ZIP
15
10
21
7
WAISTBAND 6x71 CUT 1

Indian kurtha

Kurtha is the name of the Indian shirt which men of all social classes and even some women wear. It is a lightweight, loose-fitting garment, worn outside the trousers, and has a pocket in the right side seam. It has vents at the bottom of the sides, no cuffs, and is entirely designed to be cool and airy.

Since the style is common to all people, the wearer's class and the purpose for which he has put on the garment is expressed in the choice of material – from expensive silk and handwoven linen to simple cottons. Synthetics like nylon are not suitable in the heat.

Either straight or very tight-fitting trousers are worn with the kurtha.

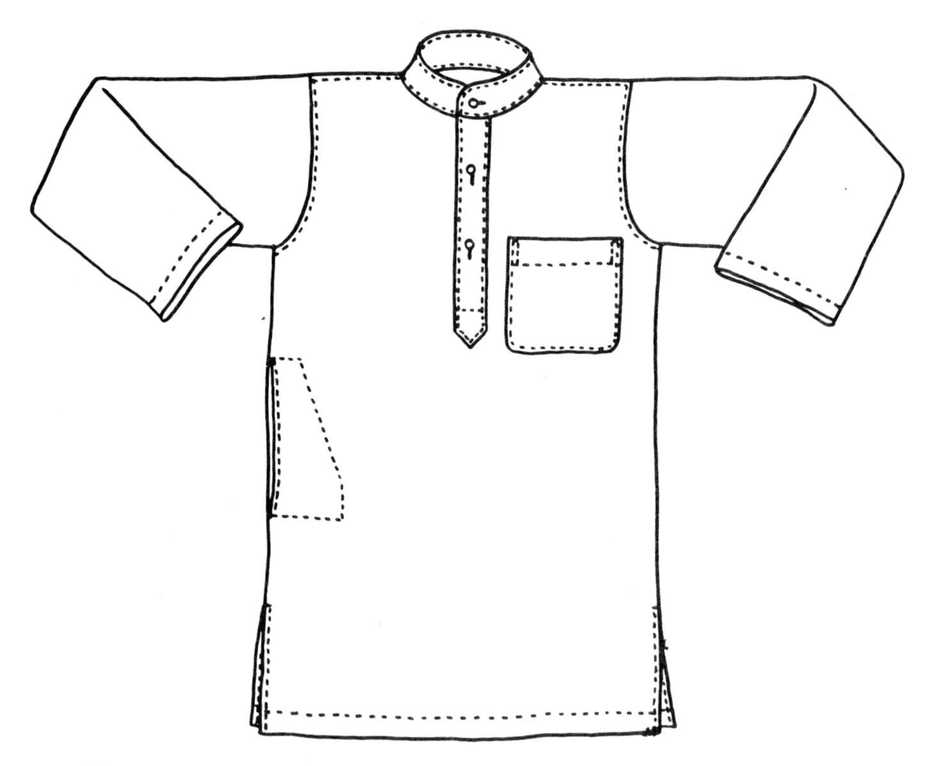

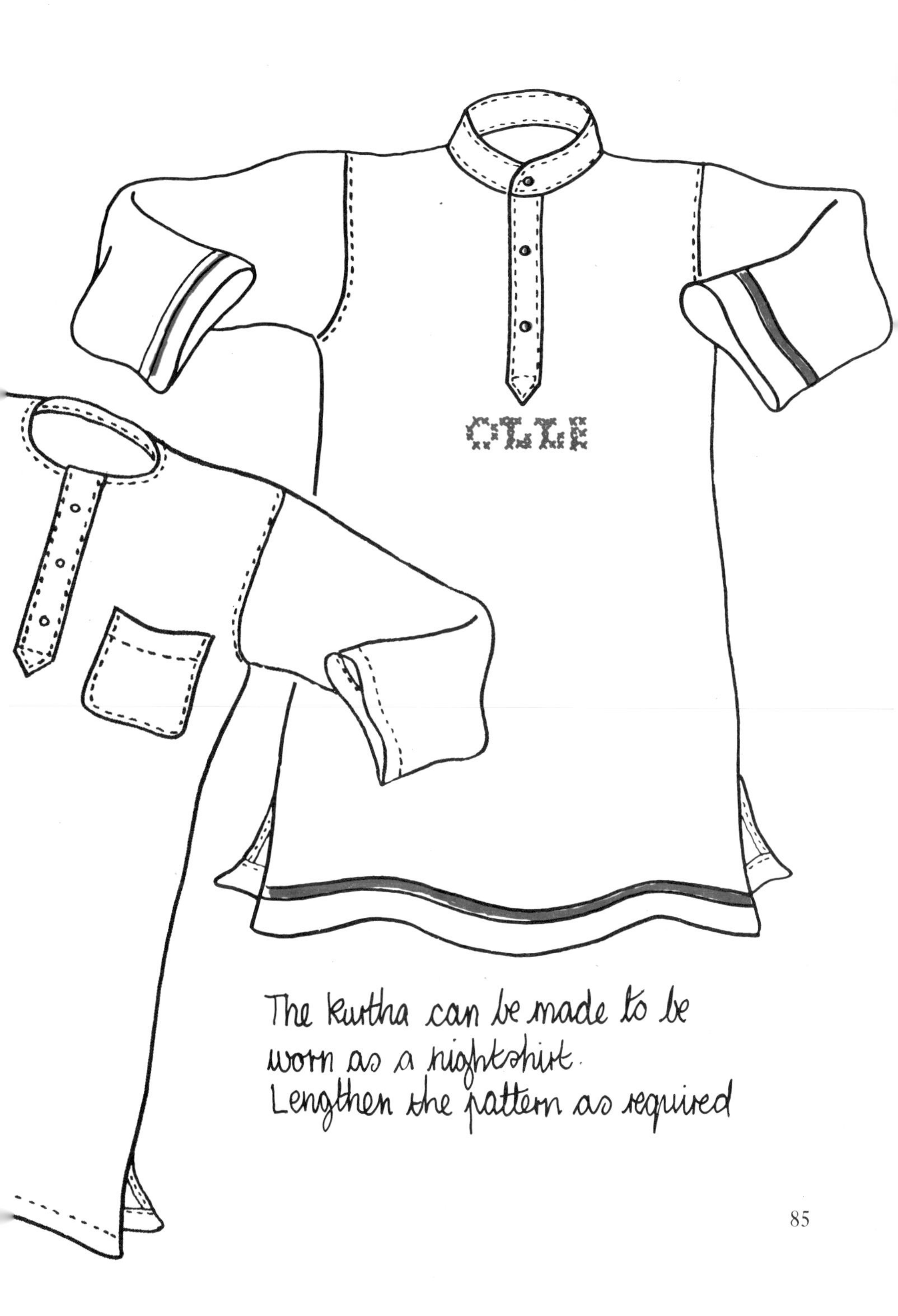
OLLE
The Kurtha can be made to be
worn as a nightshirt.
Lengthen the pattern as required

Instructions
Indian kurtha

Material required: 230 × 90 cm; three buttons.
Seam allowance: 1 cm around each piece, 3 cm at wrist and hem.

Use fine French seams (p. 14) throughout (but not on the facings).

Lay the facing on the right-hand side of the front opening, right sides together, and sew near the edge. Turn to the inside.

Take the front button band, fold and with right sides together sew the pointed end and turn it. Lay it, pointed end down, with its right side against the inside of the left-hand side of the opening. Sew close to the edge. Turn it outwards, fold in the seam allowance, and press flat. Tack to the first seam, fastening the pointed end securely.

Sew the shoulder seams with French seams. Press.

Sew the neckband, and turn it right side out. Tack one edge to the inside of the neck. Sew. Turn it up, fold in the seam allowance and press. Tack, and then top-stitch all round the collar and both sides (and the point) of the button band.

Sew the sleeves in with a fell seam, turning the seam towards the body. Press. Sew the sleeve and side seam in one go. Leave an opening in the right seam for a pocket if desired.

Hem the pocket opening. Sew the edge of the pouch to the inside of the shirt between A and B, about 5 cm below the bottom of the pocket opening. Fold as marked, and sew up the sides of the pouch. Turn under the seam allowance round the top of the pocket, and sew the pocket to the shirt from the inside.

Hem top of breast pocket, press in seam allowance all round. Tack on where marked, sew close to the edges. Hem the sleeves, side openings and bottom by machine. Make buttonholes, sew on buttons, and press the whole garment.

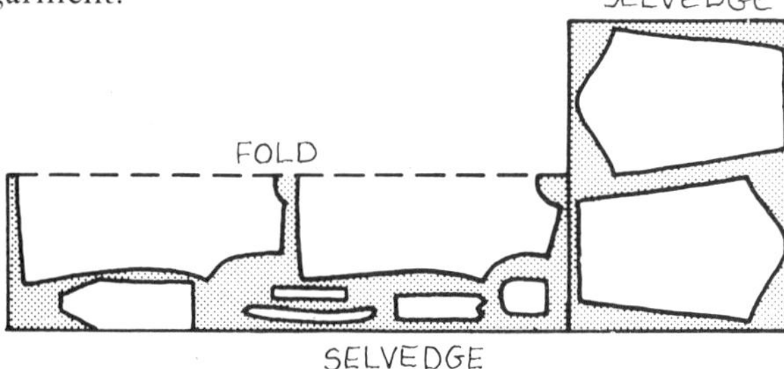

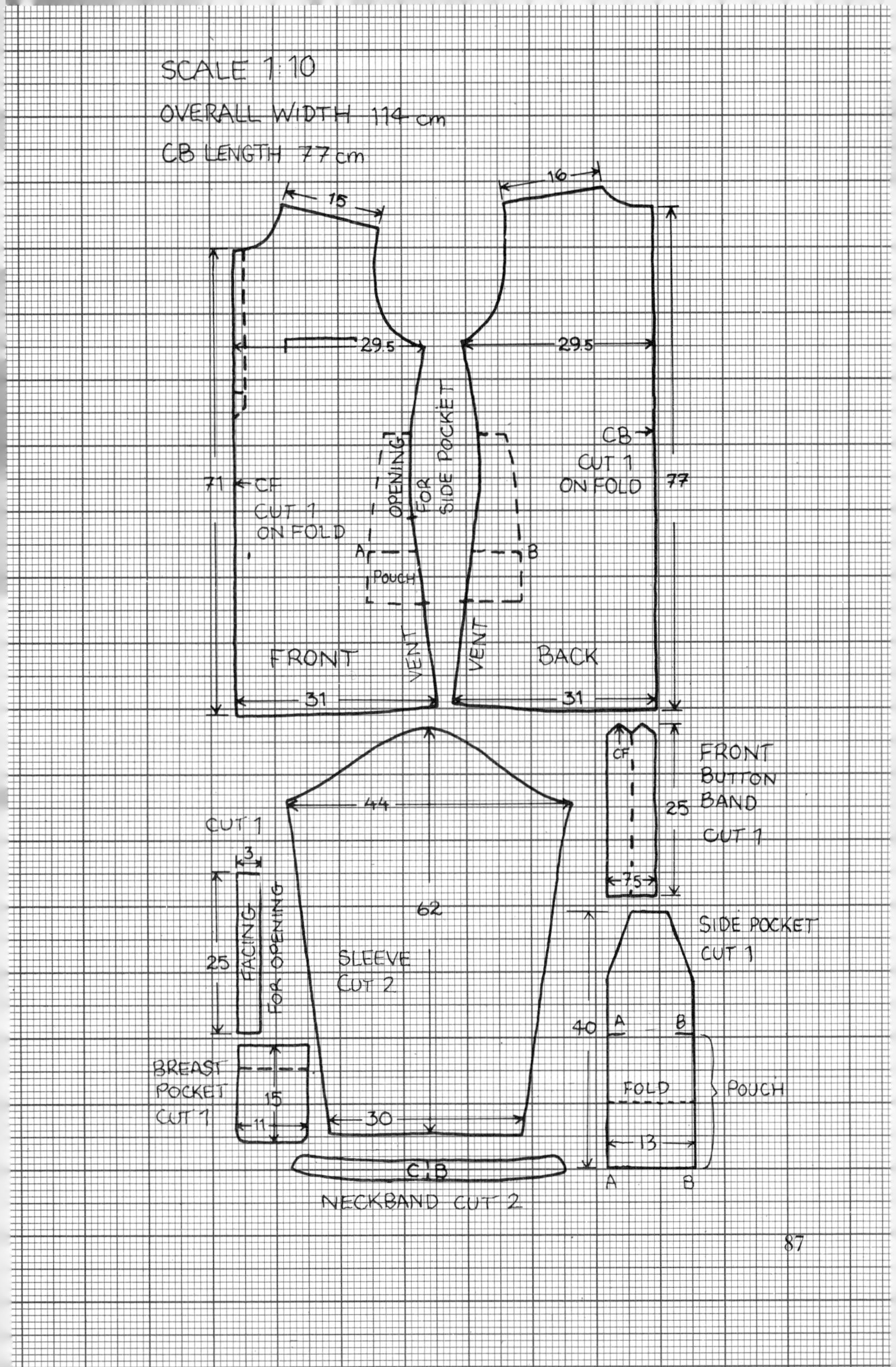

SCALE 1:10
OVERALL WIDTH 114 cm
CB LENGTH 77 cm
15
16
29.5
29.5
CB
CUT 1
ON FOLD
77
71
CF
CUT 1
ON FOLD
OPENING
FOR
SIDE POCKET
A
B
POUCH
FRONT
VENT
VENT
BACK
31
31
44
62
SLEEVE
CUT 2
30
CUT 1
3
25
FACING
FOR OPENING
BREAST
POCKET
CUT 1
15
11
C.B
NECKBAND CUT 2
CF
FRONT
BUTTON
BAND
CUT 1
25
7.5
SIDE POCKET
CUT 1
40
A
B
FOLD
POUCH
13
A
B

Bonnet

The bonnet used to be an important part of children's clothing because distinctive headgear was the easiest way of showing a baby's sex. Mothers were sometimes so concerned to make clear the sex of a baby from birth that they would sew a bonnet of each kind while still expecting. The difference in style of the two bonnets was very obvious: the girl's was sewn with a centre panel, known as a tongue, and two side pieces. The boy's was made with triangles or gussets, usually six of them.

Apart from indicating the child's sex the bonnet of course also gave protection against cold and draughts, and even served as a cushion against bumps – a necessary precaution in small, crowded, poorly heated houses.

Instructions
Bonnet

Material required: 30 × 90 cm; binding, 140 cm.
Seam allowance: 1 cm.

Sew the three pieces together, preferably with a French seam (see p. 14). Bind first the front, then the bottom edge, leaving 30 cm binding free on each end for the tie. Sew the ties and neck binding in one go. Press.

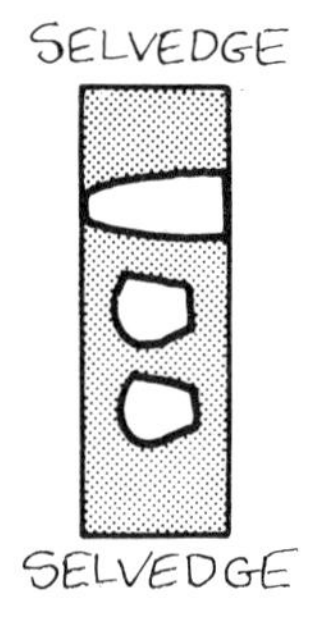

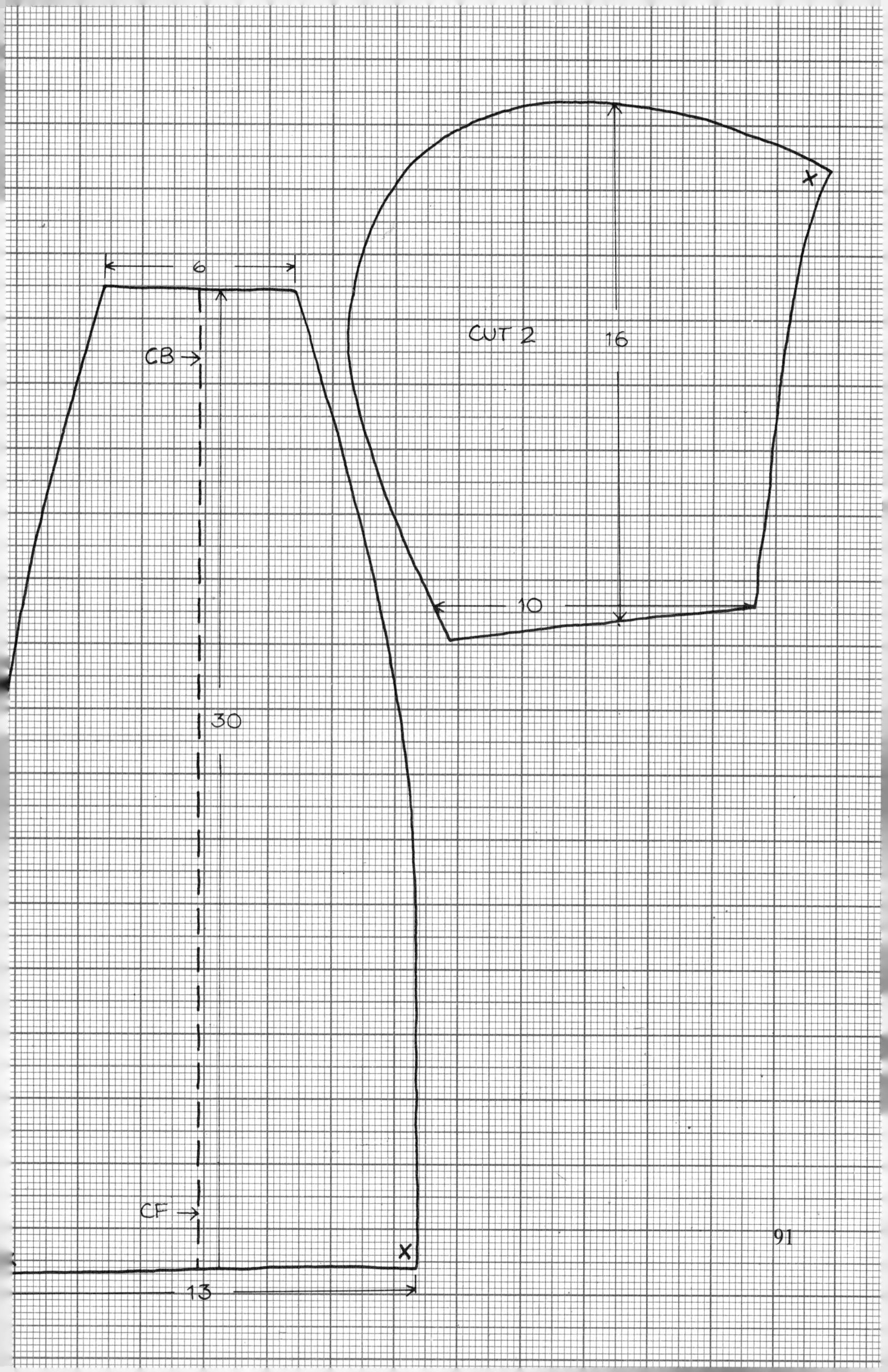
6
CB →
30
CF →
13
CUT 2
16
10

Trousers

The first trousers were just tight-fitting leggings made of skins tied with thongs, with a smock worn on top. Horsemen from Central Asia near Persia improved the design by making them out of cloth with the two legs attached to each other; and this pattern was adopted by the Greeks and Romans.

Roman legionaries on occasions wore knee-length trousers, as did the Vikings. During the early Middle Ages, however, men wore hose, i.e. long, stocking-like tubes which covered the foot completely but left the backside bare. Then when the tunic became shorter in the 1400s, the hose were sewn together with a gusset on the back, and metamorphosed into trousers.

The fantastic balloon-like breeches of the 1500s gradually grew into knee breeches, which were in use until the French Revolution in 1789. These were originally designed for noblemen horse-riding; but when the bourgeoisie took power and began to ride in carriages, they took to wearing trousers as we know them. And here the evolution stopped; carriages have become cars, but trousers have remained more or less the same.

The only change in their use is that women also wear them today, and since the First World War have taken to them increasingly wholeheartedly. This is because trousers are a fundamental, useful garment, not so susceptible to the dramatic changes on which the fashion industry thrives.

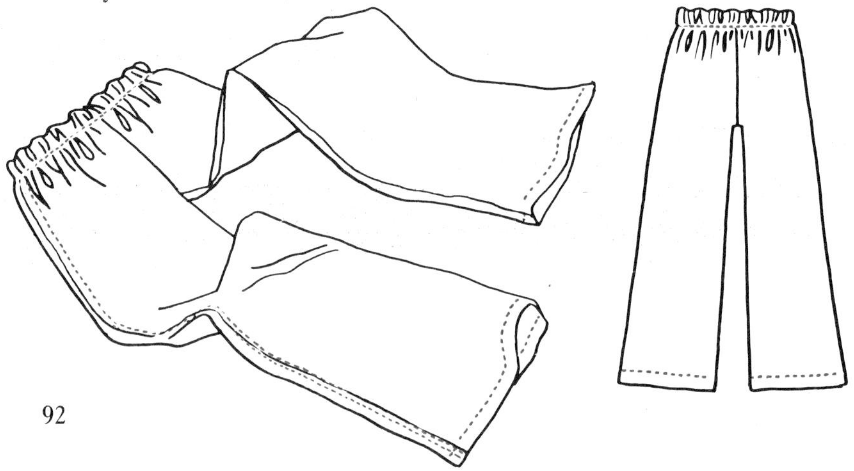

Instructions
Trousers

Material required: 250×90 cm; elastic to go round waist.
Seam allowance: 1·5 cm on the side and crotch seams, 3 cm at the waist, 5 cm at the bottom of the legs.

Sew outside leg seams. Finish them off, press forward. Then top-stitch twice from the right side, 1 mm and 1 cm from the seam. Now sew the inside leg seams. Finish and press open. Turn one trouser leg right side out, pull it into the other leg so that the inside seams are against each other, right sides together. Tack crotch seam and sew. Finish off and press. Fold in the waist, sew and thread elastic through. Hem the trouser bottoms, press.

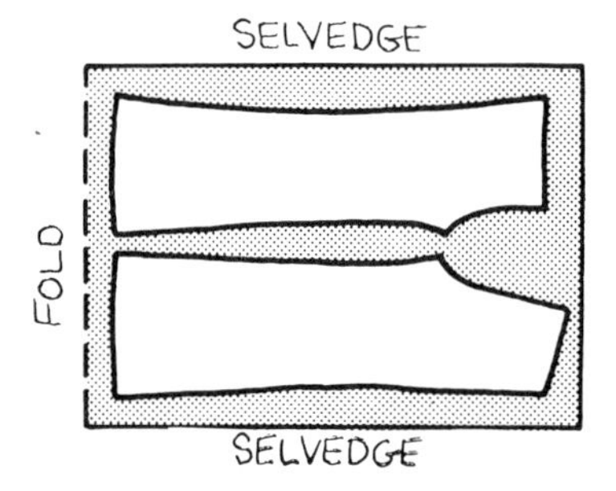

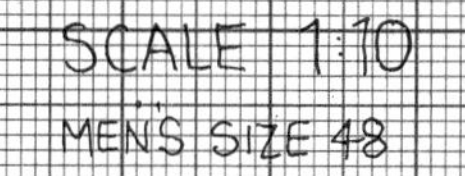
SCALE 1:10
MEN'S SIZE 48

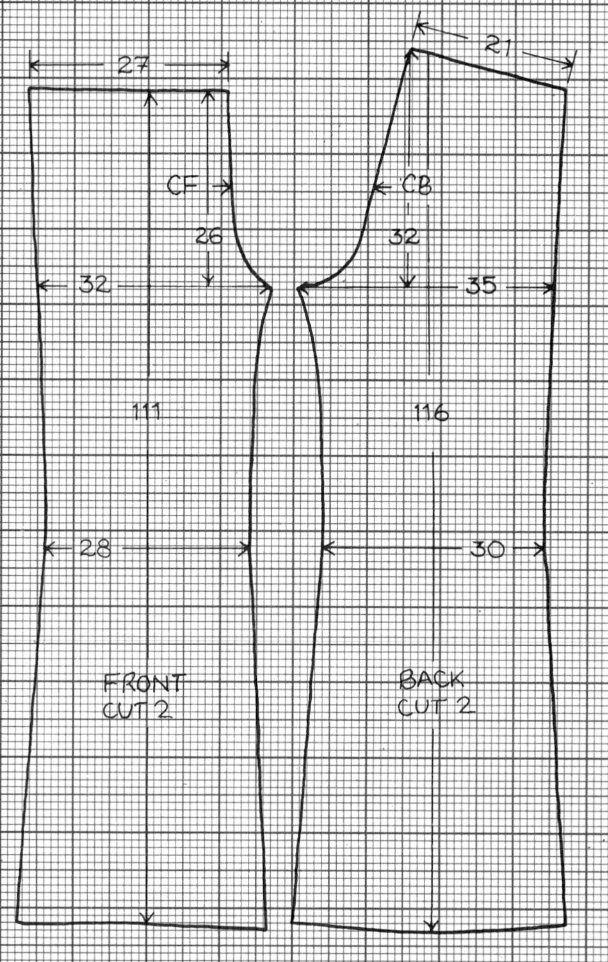
27
CF
26
32
111
28
FRONT
CUT 2
21
CB
32
35
116
30
BACK
CUT 2

Butterfly tunic

The butterfly tunic is a long top worn over trousers or skirt by men and women in most parts of Africa. It can be full length, and then serves as a dress. A length of fabric is taken and sewn down the sides of the body some way in from the edge of the cloth so that the outer part will float freely. Printed fabrics with symmetrical patterns and border prints are used for both skirt and top, which makes the whole outfit look like a painting in a frame.

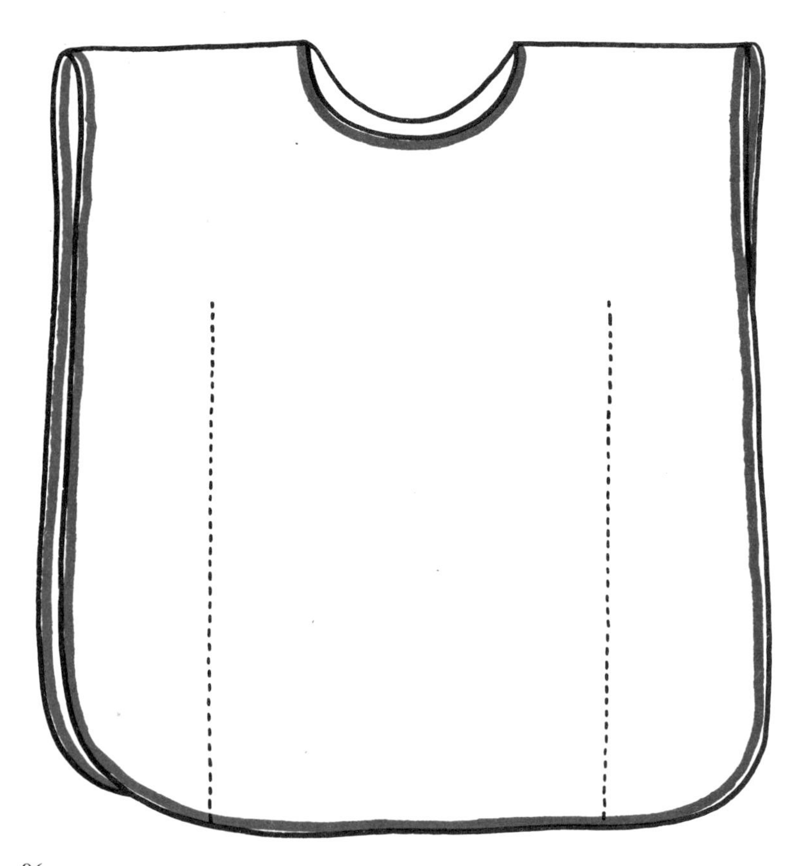

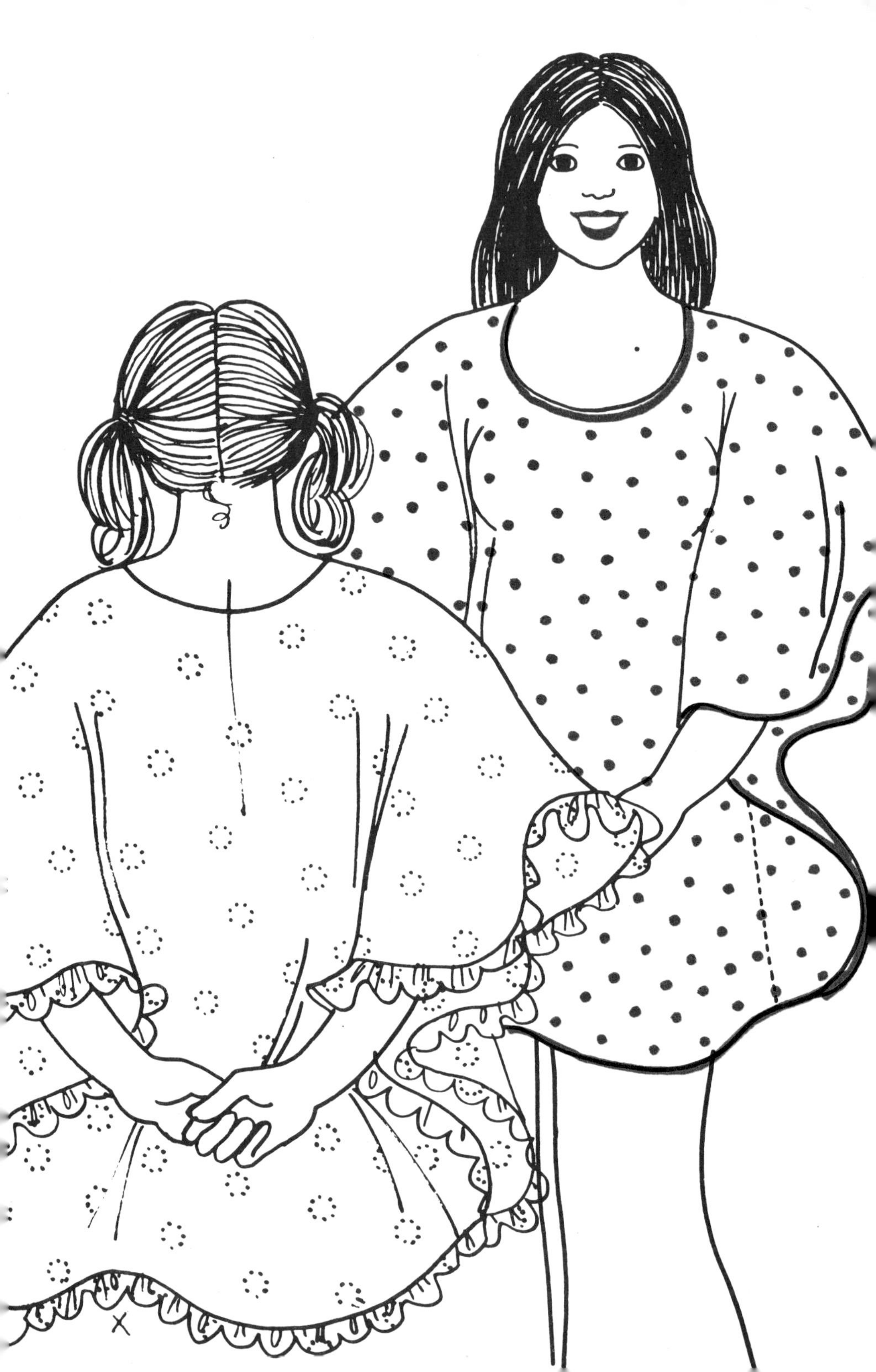

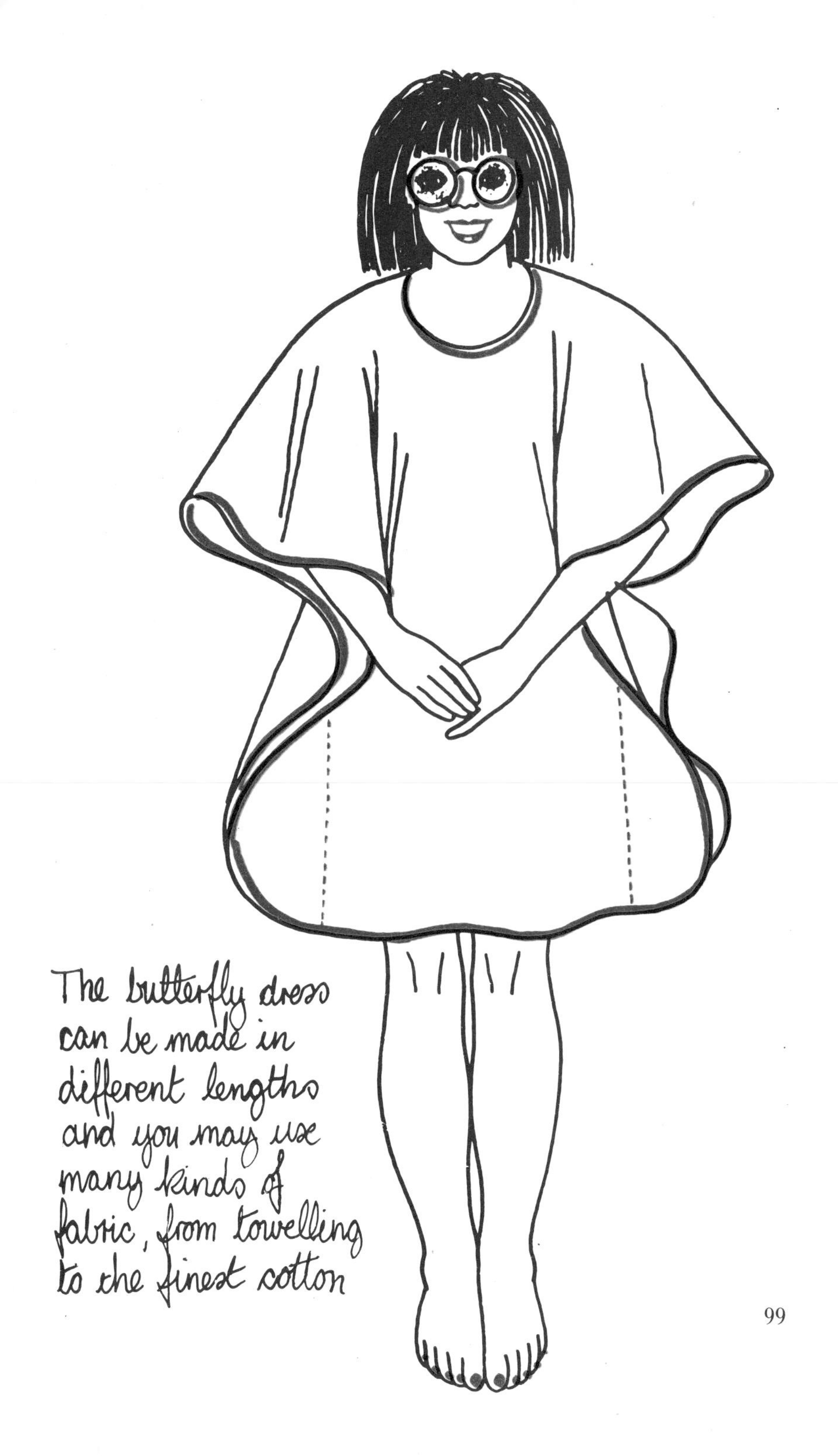
The butterfly dress
can be made in
different lengths
and you may use
many kinds of
fabric, from towelling
to the finest cotton

Instructions
Butterfly tunic

Material required: 160 × 90 cm; 540 cm bias binding (see p. 15).

Cut out a hole for the head and bind it. Bind all round the garment edges. Press. Fold the garment with the right side out, and sew front and back together from the right side, as marked, allowing as much room as you want. Press.

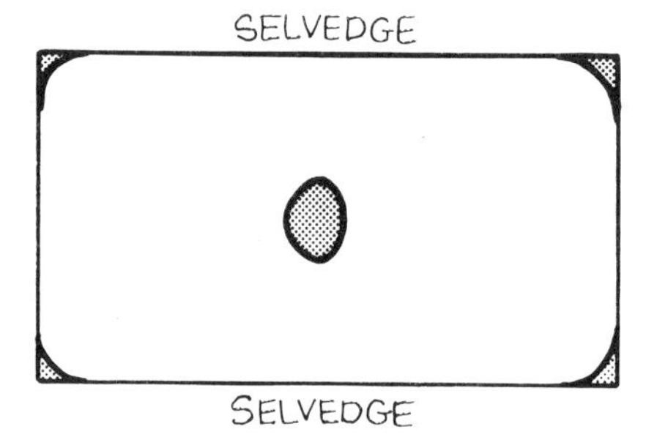

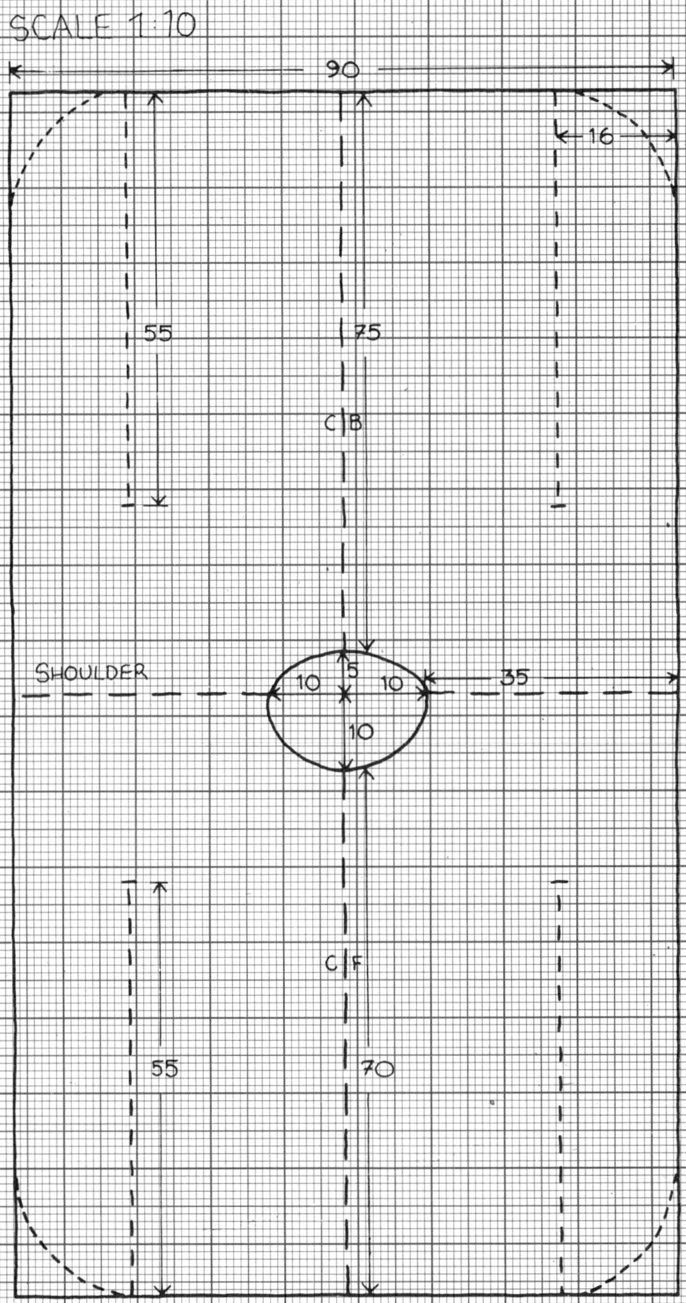

SCALE 1:10

90

16

55

75

C B

SHOULDER

10

5

10

35

10

C F

55

70

American Indian top

For hundreds of years the North American Indians on the prairies wore a skin shirt resembling a poncho. It consisted of two skins sewn together at the shoulders and hanging loose at the sides. There was a head hole and a slash at the neck covered by a characteristic triangular 'bib'. The women's dress was much the same as the men's shirt, only longer.

The material was usually deerskin treated so that it was soft and beautiful. The hair was scraped off, the fat from the animal's liver and brains rubbed into it, and the skin then left to soak in water for several days. Then it was wrung and spread out, dried and stretched out on ropes and rubbed with a cudgel. Lastly it was smoked over a slow fire to give it colour and make it stay soft.

In the 1800s the garment was sewn together at the sides, although the skins' natural shape was still not trimmed. The shirt also acquired its unique decoration of fringes and bead embroidery. To this were added the skin leggings, moccasins and fantastic feather headdress.

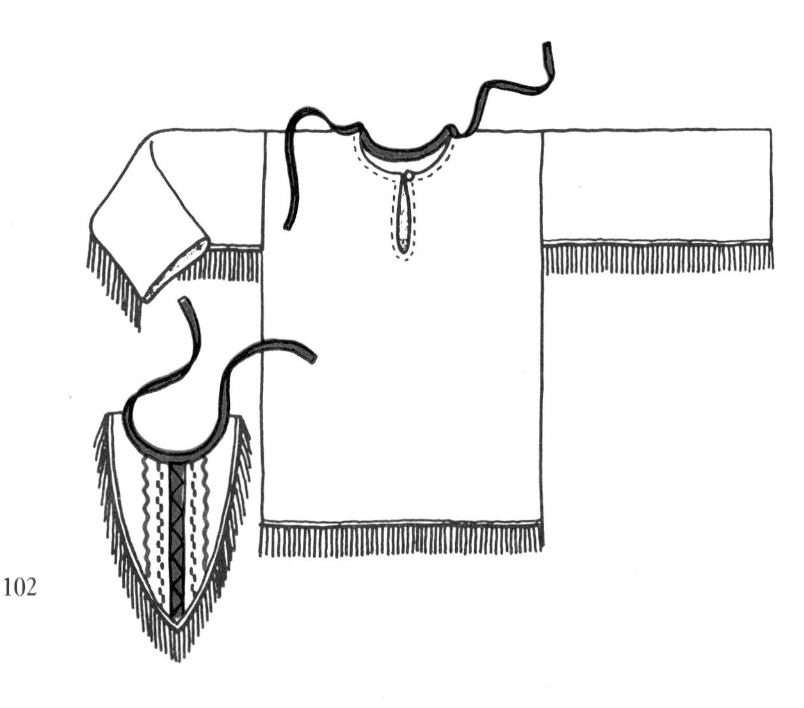

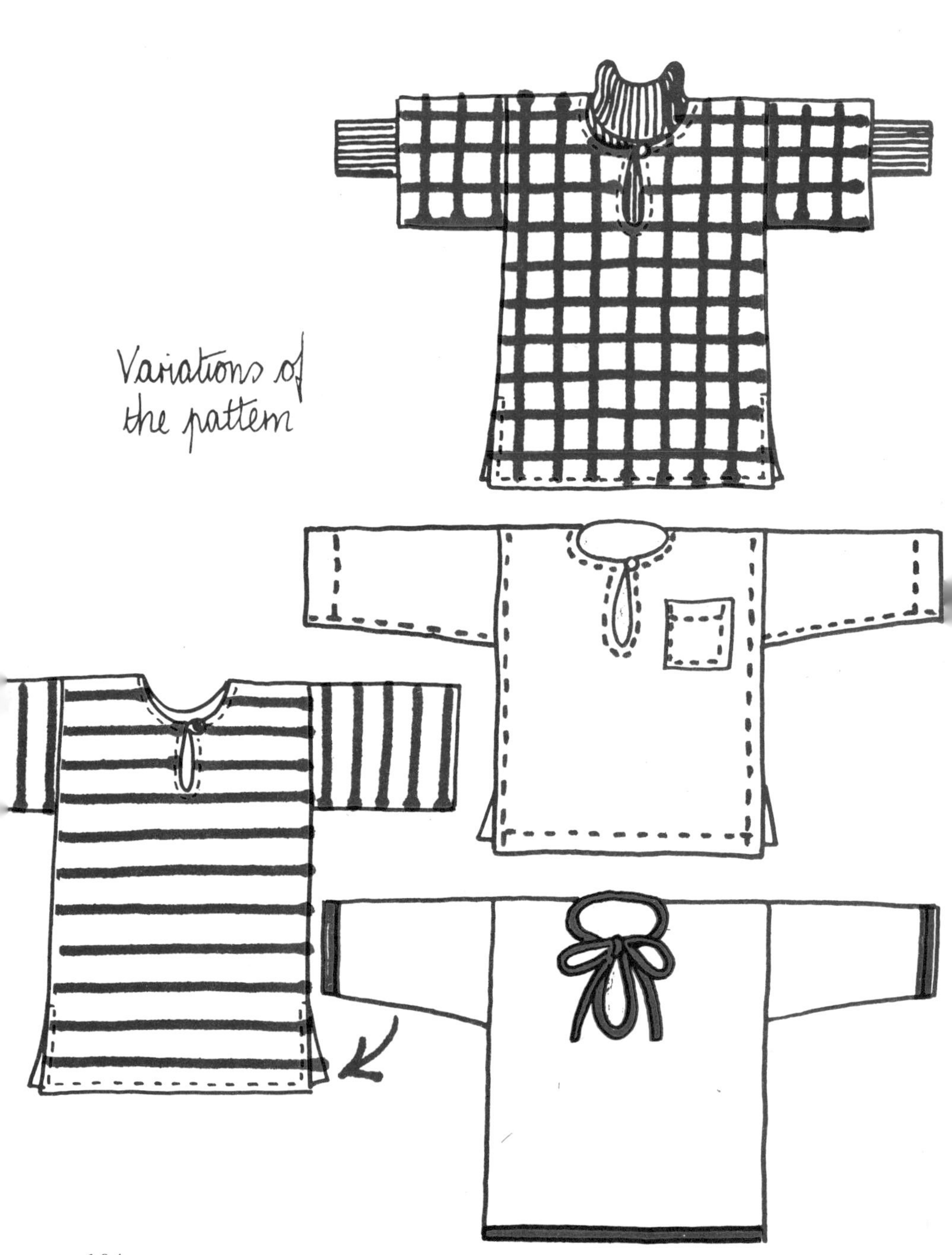
Variations of
the pattern

Instructions
American Indian top

Material required (adult): 215 × 90 cm; fringe, 260 cm; bias binding, 175 cm.
Material required (child): 110 × 90 cm; fringe, 210 cm; bias binding, 165 cm.
Seam allowance: 1 cm round each piece, 3 cm at wrist and hem.

Lay the neck facing on the main piece, right sides together, and sew around the neck and front opening. Cut the opening and trim the turning at the point close to the seam; turn to the inside and press. Turn under the edges of the facing. Top-stitch 7 mm from the edge round neck and front opening.

Attach sleeves as marked. Lay fringe over the seams on the right side and sew it on. Sew the arm and side seams in one go. Leave an opening at the bottom. Finish off seams.

Hem the shirt by machine at the bottom and wrists. Strengthen the underarm with an extra row of stitching on the outside. Sew the fringe on round the bottom.

Sew and turn the bib. Press. Embroider with braid and beads. Sew fringe on the sides of the bib, and bind the neck edge, leaving 25 cm of bias binding loose at either end for ties. Bind the shirt neck at the back leaving ties 25 cm long at each side. Press.

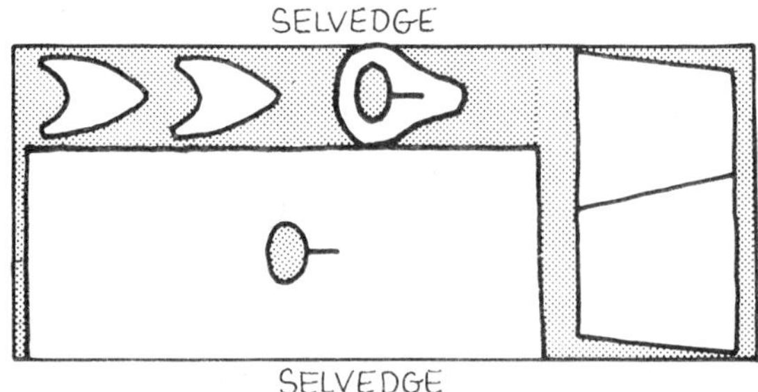

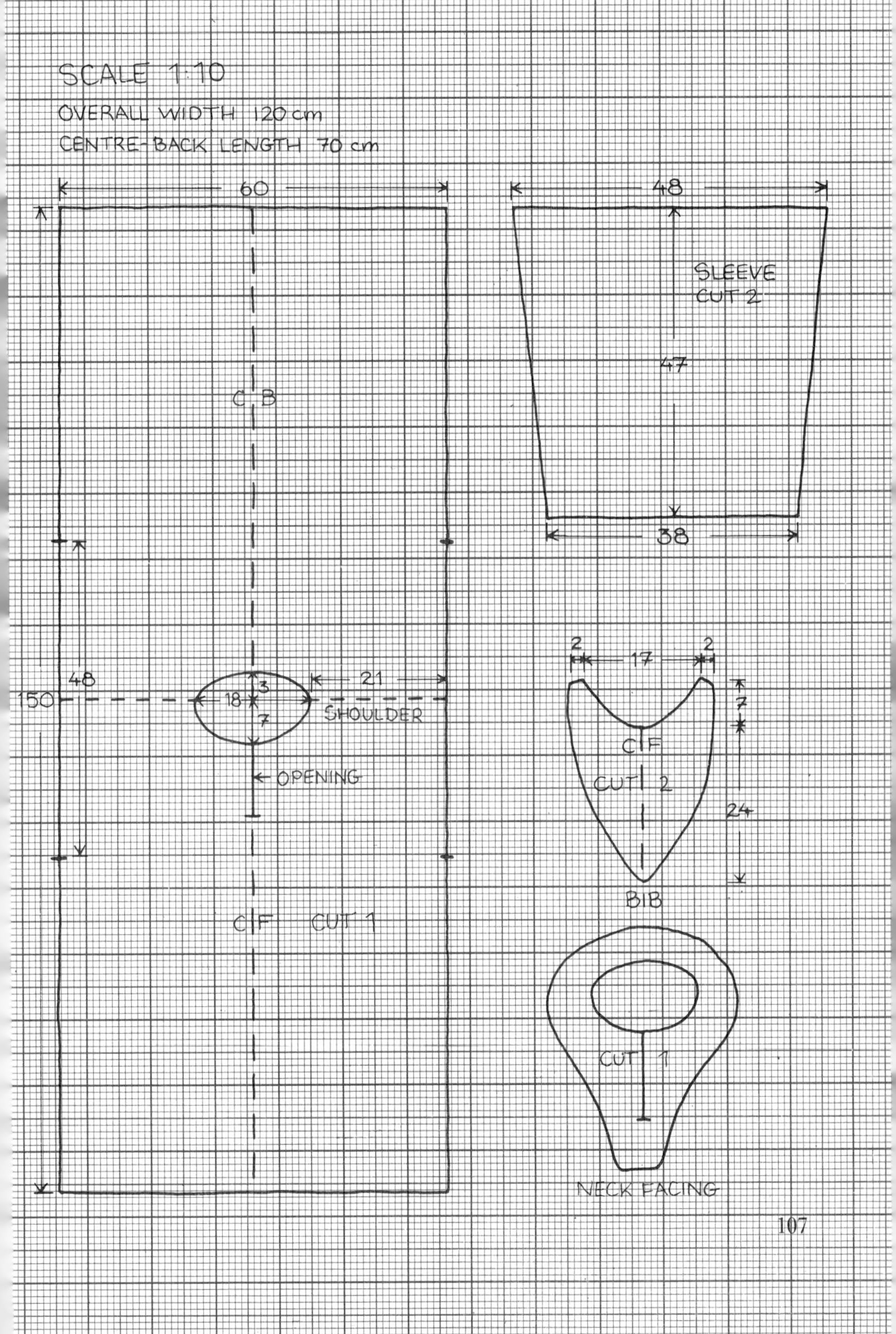
SCALE 1:10
OVERALL WIDTH 120 cm
CENTRE-BACK LENGTH 70 cm
60
C B
150
48
18
3
7
21
SHOULDER
OPENING
C F
CUT 1
48
SLEEVE
CUT 2
47
38
2
17
2
7
24
C F
CUT 2
BIB
CUT 1
NECK FACING

American Indian top – child's size

See p. 106 for the materials required and the instructions for making up.

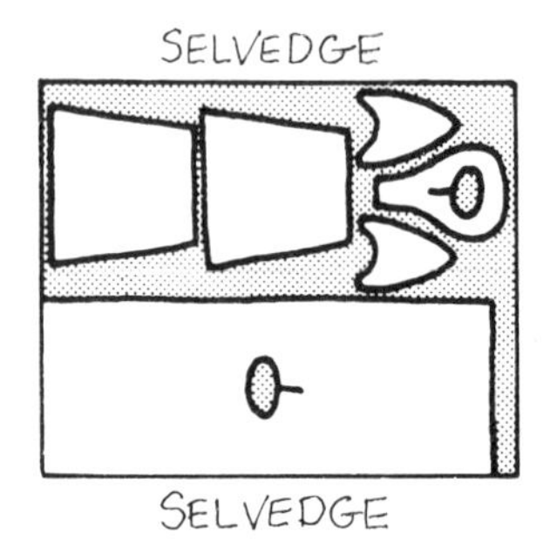

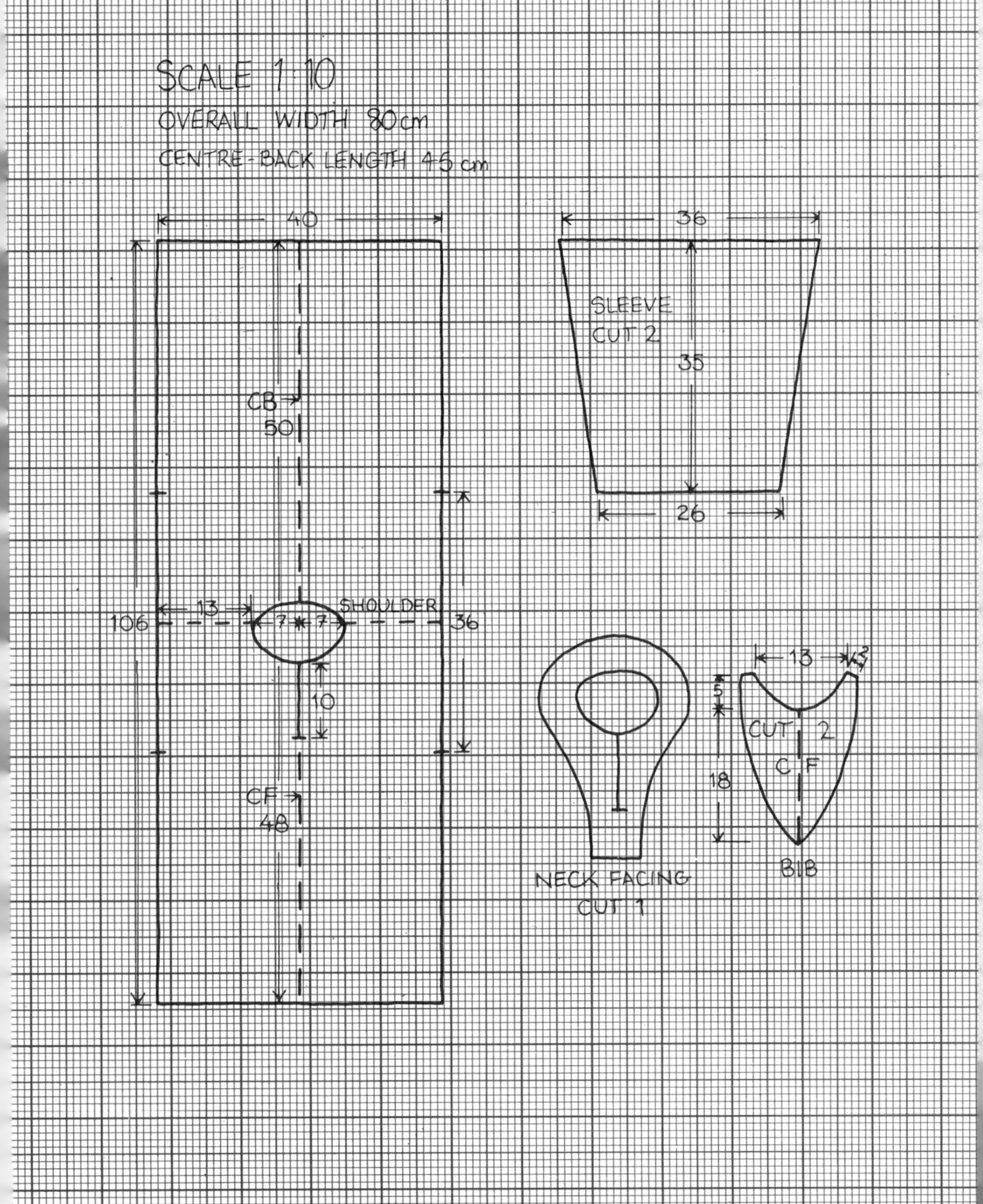
SCALE 1:10
OVERALL WIDTH 80cm
CENTRE-BACK LENGTH 45 cm
40
CB
50
13
SHOULDER
7
7
106
36
10
CF
48
36
SLEEVE
CUT 2
35
26
NECK FACING
CUT 1
13
2
5
CUT 2
C F
18
BIB

Waistcoat

The waistcoat was once a long garment worn under a long coat. Little by little it grew shorter and the arms disappeared. The waistcoat in this book does not even have buttons. But it has regained its former length and is adapted as topwear for women.

Instructions
Waistcoat

Material required: 130×90 cm; bias binding, 600 cm.
Seam allowance: 2 cm at centre back and side and shoulder seams, 1 cm round the pocket, nothing at the front edge, neck or armholes if the garment is to be bound with bias binding; otherwise 1 cm.

Sew bust darts. Sew centre-back seam, and the side and shoulder seams. Try on, adjust if necessary. Press seams open.

Hem the top of the pocket, press the seam allowances in. Tack to the waistcoat as marked. Sew close to the edge.

Open one edge of the folded bias binding, tack to the inside of the front edge round the whole waistcoat. Sew and turn it to the right side. Press. Sew the binding down on the right side close to its edge.

Bind the neck and leave enough at both ends for ties. Bind the armholes, beginning from the side seams.

If you want hand-sewn rouleaux binding, sew the bias binding to the waistcoat by machine, right sides together. Turn the bias to the inside, then sew by hand with small neat stitches along the line of the machine stitching. Press.

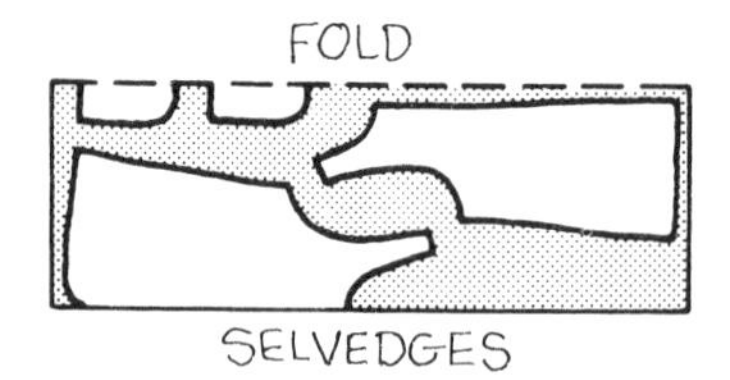

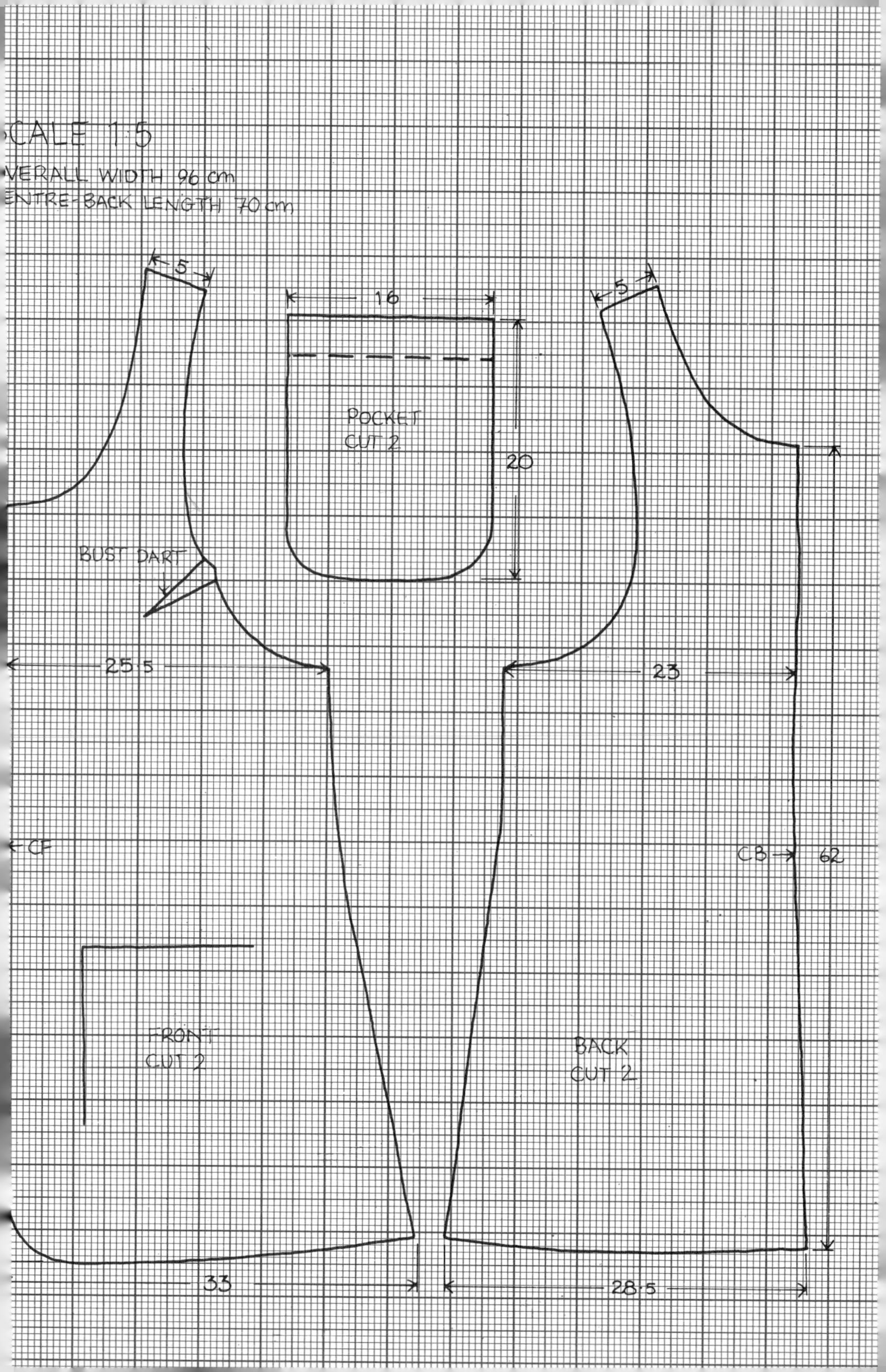
SCALE 1:5
OVERALL WIDTH 96 cm
CENTRE-BACK LENGTH 70 cm
5
16
5
POCKET
CUT 2
20
BUST DART
25·5
23
CF
CB
62
FRONT
CUT 2
BACK
CUT 2
33
28·5

Ruana

This garment is called a *ruana* in Colombia, a *luipil* in Mexico, and has other names in other parts of the world. A straight poncho made from a length of material with a hole for the head. That is all.

If it is made in wool and left open at the sides it may be worn by men and women, as an overgarment, as it is in Colombia. Or it can be in fine cotton, sewn at the sides with openings for the arms and worn on its own by women, as it is in Mexico. It never has either collar or sleeves. The richness of materials and colours and simple but meaningful variations at the neck opening make the garment very individual. Coloured fabrics are probably the easiest to use for good results.

Full-length ruana
made in blanketing

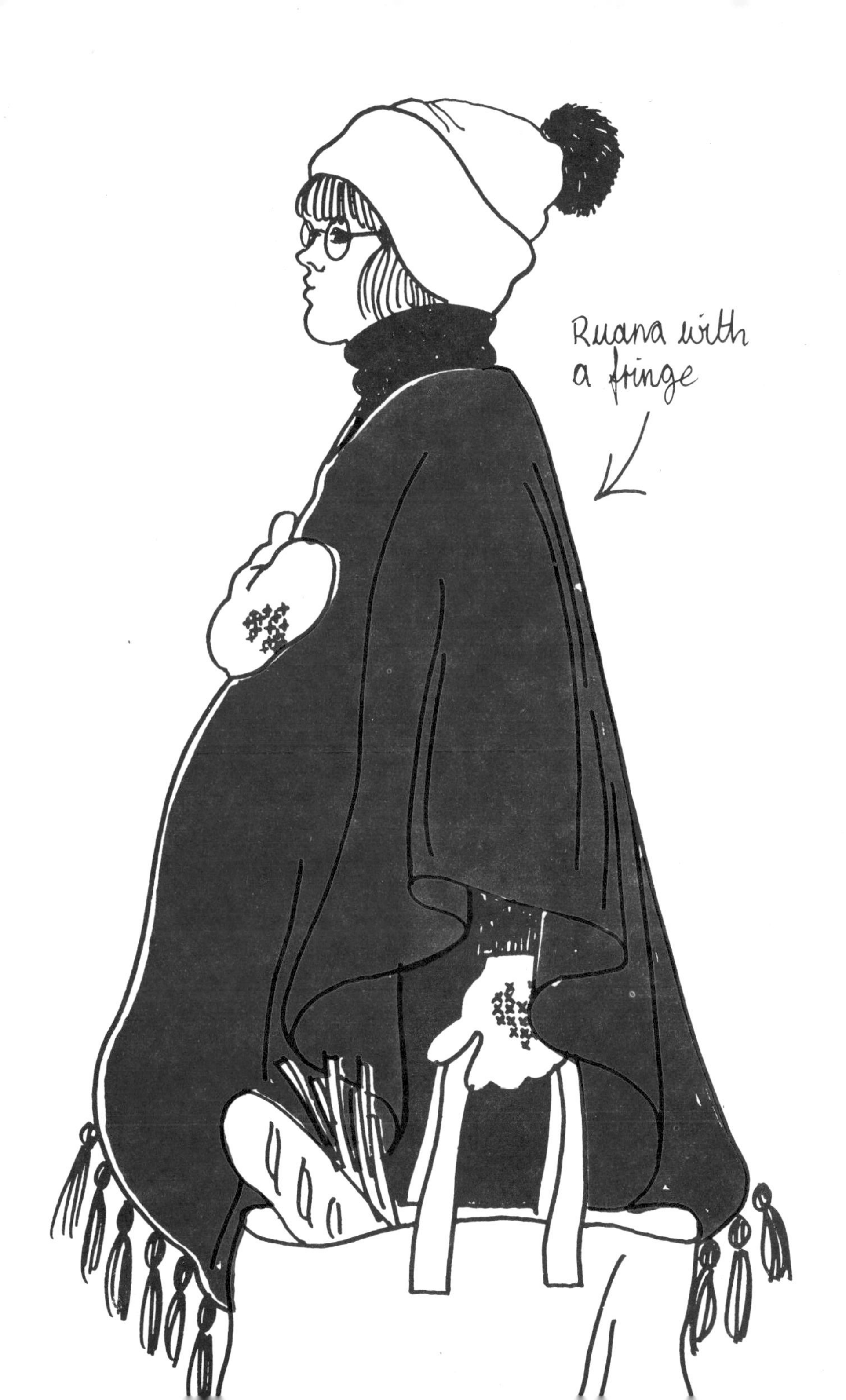
Ruana with a fringe

Instructions
Ruana

Material required: 180 × 195 cm; 250 cm fringe.

Fold the piece of material and sew a fringe along the shorter sides. Cut a slash in the middle as marked. Crochet or blanket stitch round the neck.

Easiest of all is a ruana made of wool plaid with the edges frayed to make the fringe.

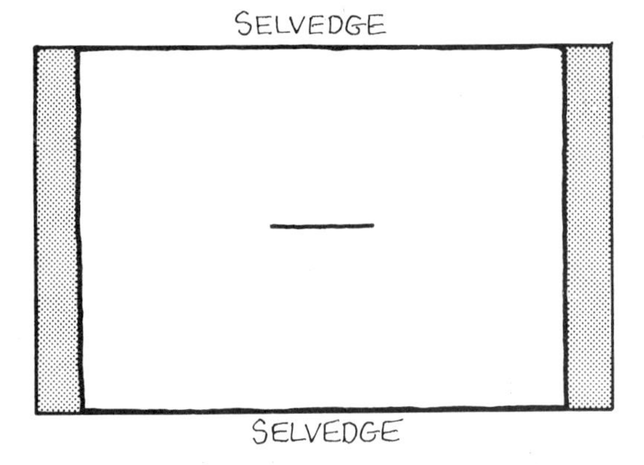

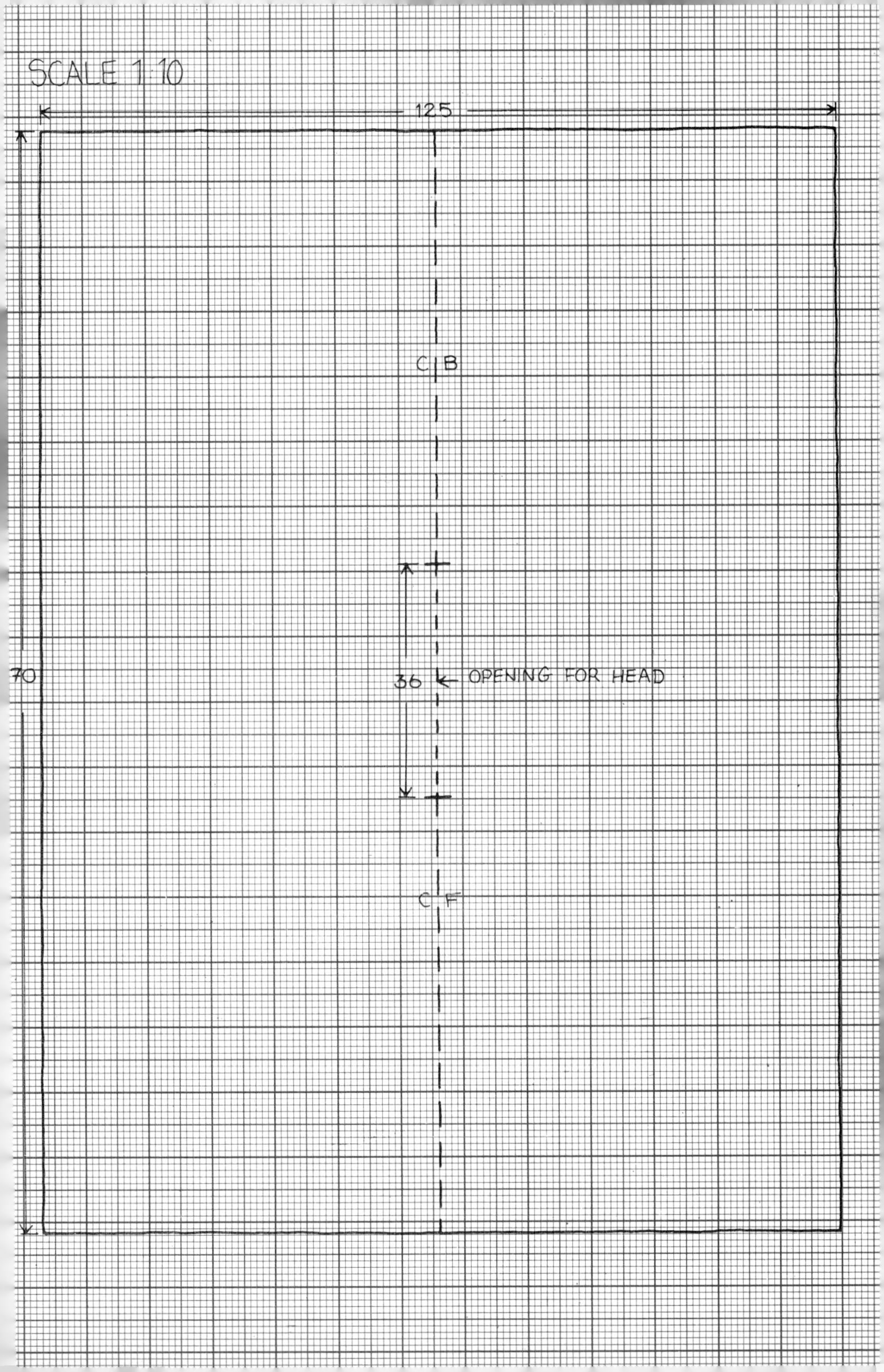
SCALE 1:10
125
70
C B
36
OPENING FOR HEAD
C F

Duffel coat

The English duffel coat was a utility creation of the Second World War. General Montgomery wore it when fighting the Desert War against the Germans, and it was also standard issue in the British Navy. It then spread over the Western World with the film *The Third Man*, in which Trevor Howard played a British military policeman in a duffel coat.

It is a useful coat, simple and very light since it has no lining, but still warm, being made of thick, blanket-like wool which comes from the Dutch town of Duffel in Brabant. The style has military features, such as the flat overlapping front and the loop fastenings with toggles. The hood may have been taken from the monk's habit. It is a straightforward and very useful garment.

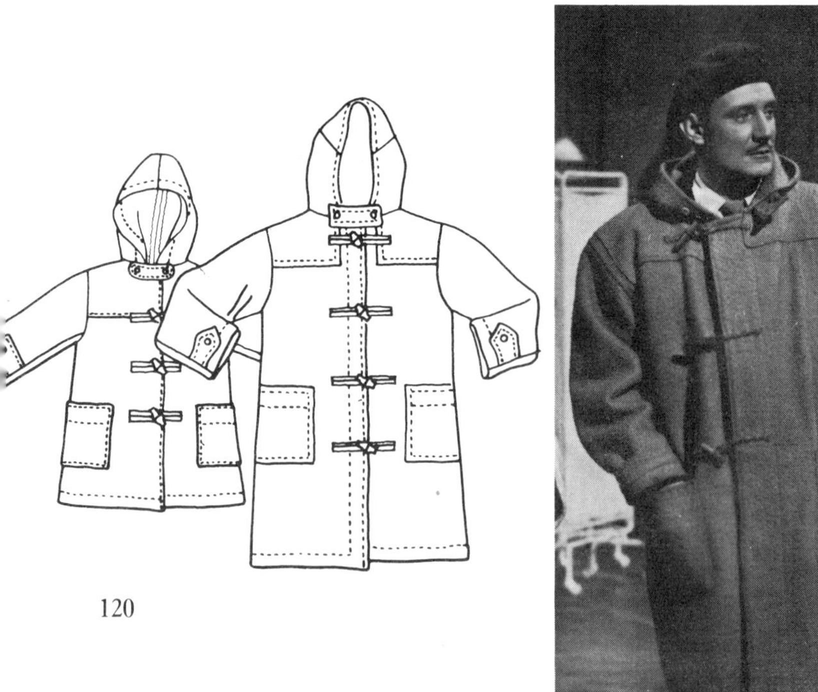

Instructions
Duffel coat

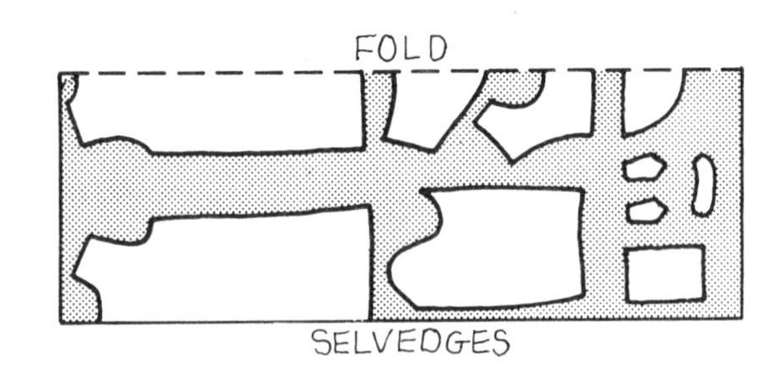

Material required: 220 × 150 cm; heavy cotton thread for top-stitching; toggles; cord for loops.
Seam allowance: 1·5 cm all round the sleeve and side seams, 1 cm round all other parts, 4 cm at the cuffs and round the front edge of the hood, 5 cm at the coat hem.

Lay front and back pieces right sides together and sew side seams. Lay the shoulder seams wrong sides together and sew. (The raw edges will be on the outside.)

Sew the button bands and turn them right side out. Then press and top-stitch 12 mm from the edge all the way round them. Attach them according to the markings into the sleeve seams. Sew the sleeve seams. Sew a double row of gathering stitches round the top of the arm to help in easing the sleeves in.

Press all seams open and press the side seams towards the centre back. Tack the sleeves in and try the coat on, adjusting if necessary. Undo the tacking.

Finish all seams except the shoulder seams. Top-stitch a 12 mm wide decorative seam with thicker cotton from the right side along the side seams.

Sew the two hood pieces together. Finish the seam. Fold in the front facing and top-stitch with heavy cotton 12 mm from the edge. Pin the hood to the neck of the coat, wrong sides together. Turn the front facings in along the fold line.

Turn in the seam allowances of the yoke at the bottom and centre fronts, and tack. Lay the yoke over the hood, right sides together, with the centre-back marks matching up. Tack everything firmly together and machine right round the neck. Turn the yoke down and press. Tack the yoke edges to the front and back and top-stitch from the right side. The yoke now covers the shoulder seams.

Tack the sleeves into the body and sew. Finish the seams. Hem the sleeves. Top-stitch 12 mm in around the cuffs.

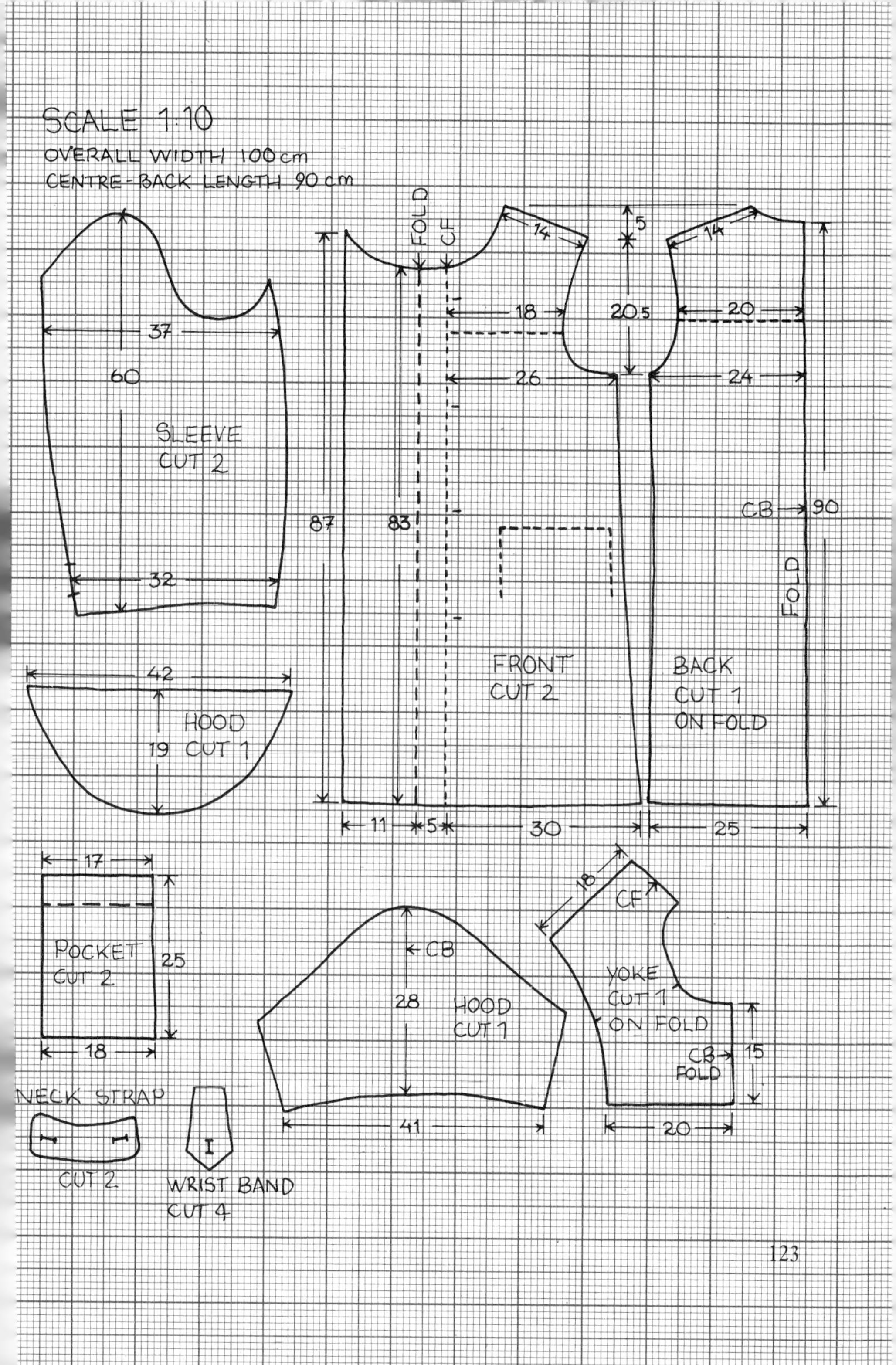
SCALE 1:10
OVERALL WIDTH 100 cm
CENTRE-BACK LENGTH 90 cm
SLEEVE
CUT 2
37
60
32
42
HOOD
CUT 1
19
FOLD
CF
14
5
18
20.5
20
26
24
87
83
CB
90
FOLD
FRONT
CUT 2
BACK
CUT 1
ON FOLD
11
5
30
25
17
POCKET
CUT 2
25
18
18
CF
CB
28
HOOD
CUT 1
41
YOKE
CUT 1
ON FOLD
CB
FOLD
15
20
NECK STRAP
CUT 2
WRIST BAND
CUT 4

Finish the bottom hem edge and turn up. Top-stitch 12 mm from the front edge. Top-stitch again 4·5 cm in from that all the way down the front and along the bottom hem.

Fold in the top of the pockets, turning in the seam allowance at the sides, and sew. Press in the seam allowances all round pockets and sew on as marked. Sew and turn the neck strap. Sew buttonholes and buttons for the button bands, sew toggles and loops on the coat front. Press.

Instructions

Child's duffel

Material required: 125 × 140 cm; heavy cotton thread for top-stitching; toggles; cord for loops.
Seam allowance: 1 cm around neck, hood, armhole, top of sleeve and pocket, 1·5 cm on shoulder and side seams, 4 cm at cuffs, 6 cm for the front facing.

Sew the wristbands and turn them right side out. Top-stitch, and attach to the sleeve seam as marked. Place the top sleeve on the under sleeve, right sides together, and sew the sleeve seams. Press the seams open. Sew two rows of gathering stitches round the top of the arm to help ease the sleeve into the armhole.

Sew the side seams and finish. Press towards the back. Sew the shoulder seams with the raw edges to the right side. Press open. Sew the two pieces of the hood together and press the seam open. Fold in the front edge of the hood and top-stitch from the right side 2·5 cm from the edge.

Tack in one sleeve and the hood and try the garment on. Undo the tacking and make any adjustments necessary. Press in the front edges of the coat.

Lay the hood on the coat, wrong sides together, and pin. Then place the yoke on the hood, right sides together, and tack securely along the neckline. Sew the neck seam all round. Turn the yoke right side out and press. Turn in the seam allowances at the bottom edge of the yoke, front and back, and at the centre front. Press. Top-stitch through yoke and coat from the right side. Tack in the sleeves, and sew. Finish seams.

SCALE 1:10

HEIGHT 115 cm

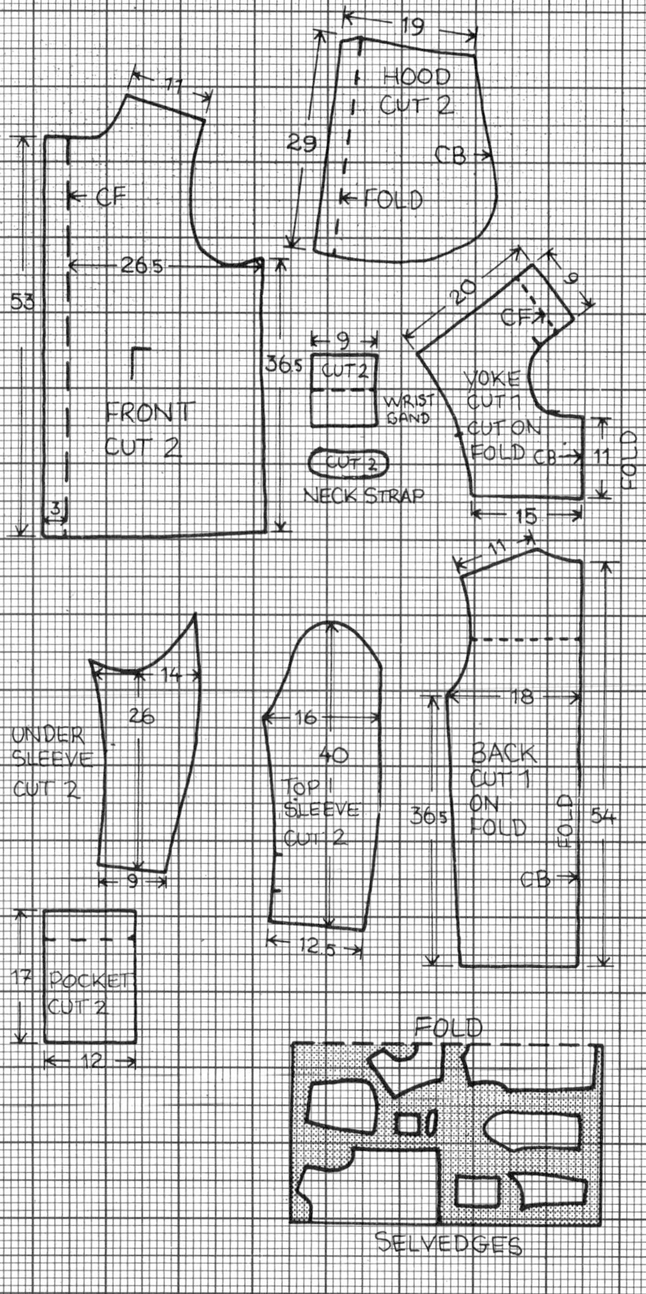

HOOD
CUT 2
19
29
CB
FOLD

FRONT
CUT 2
11
CF
26.5
53
36.5
3

CUT 2
9
WRIST BAND

CUT 2
NECK STRAP

YOKE
CUT 1
CUT ON
FOLD
20
9
CF
CB
11
15
FOLD

UNDER
SLEEVE
CUT 2
14
26
9

TOP
SLEEVE
CUT 2
16
40
12.5

BACK
CUT 1
ON
FOLD
11
18
36.5
54
FOLD
CB

POCKET
CUT 2
17
12

FOLD
SELVEDGES

Girl's pinafore

At the end of the nineteenth century it was common for children to wear pinafores, both for everyday and smart wear. Sometimes girls had elaborately embroidered ones with pin tucks and lace which were a status symbol for children from better-off homes. Indeed, the pinafore could be a beautiful garment in white lawn, almost like a dress. It is a garment which is worth reviving.

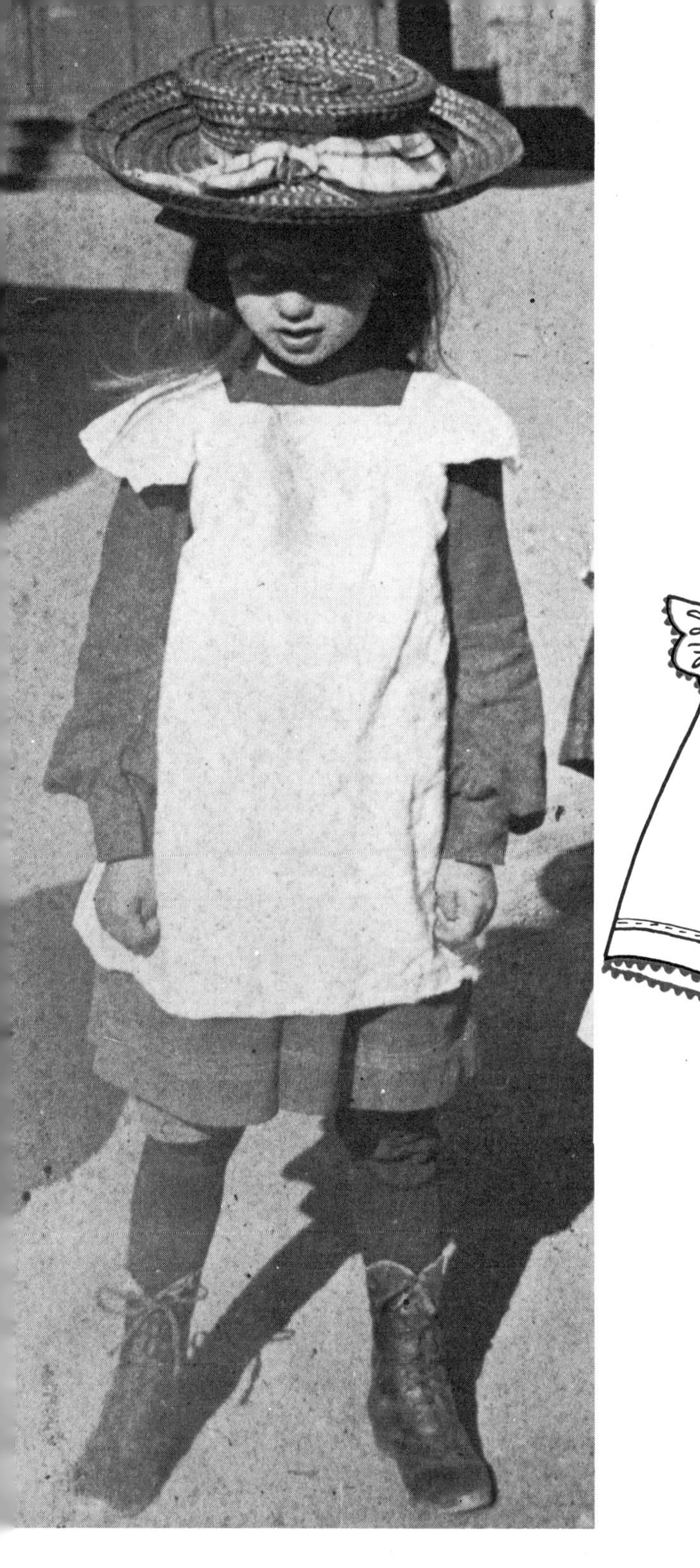

Instructions
Girl's pinafore

Material required: 75 × 90 cm (if you use lace for the yoke you will need slightly less); 350 cm rick-rack braid; 1 m lace 4 cm wide for yoke, if desired; 150 cm bias binding; 2 buttons.
Seam allowance: 1 cm around each piece.

Mark and sew pin tucks. Press them outwards, starting from the middle. Sew centre-back seam up to the opening marks.

Hem the outer edge of the frills by machine with a very narrow turning, and sew on the rick-rack braid. Sew a double row of gathering stitches on the inner edge.

Make the yoke either of lace or of two thicknesses of cloth. Make yoke and yoke facing by joining the shoulder straps to the back and front yokes at the slanting edges. Press the seams open. Lay the yoke pieces against each other, right sides together, and sew the neck edge. Turn and press. Press in seam allowances on the outside edge, tack the body to the yoke and tack the rick-rack braid on the seam. Sew from the right side.

Attach the gathered frills to the shoulders, right sides together. Let the frills extend 2 cm below the yoke and bodice seam.

Sew the sides with French seams. Finish off the facing to the yoke on the inside with bias binding. Slip-stitch the yoke. Hem the bottom by machine. Sew rick-rack braid round the hem and neck. Sew on a narrow bias strip as marked above the hem. Sew two buttons and loops to the back of the yoke. Press.

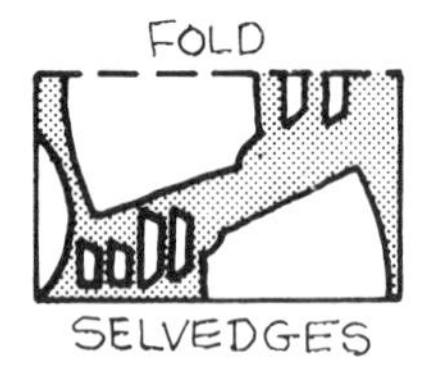

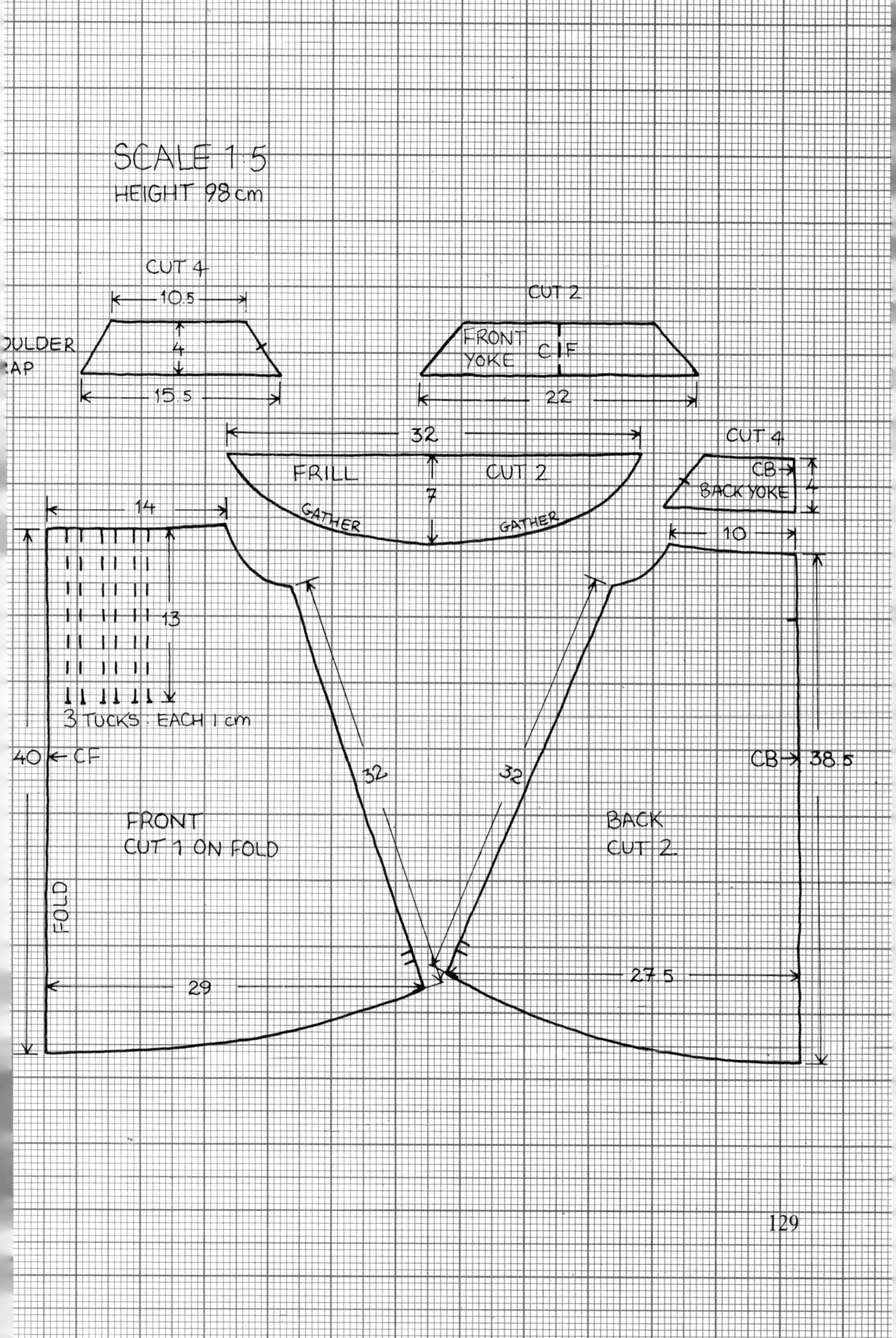
SCALE 1:5
HEIGHT 98 cm
CUT 4
10.5
4
15.5
OULDER
AP
CUT 2
FRONT
YOKE
C F
22
32
FRILL
CUT 2
7
GATHER
GATHER
CUT 4
CB
BACK YOKE
4
10
14
13
3 TUCKS : EACH 1 cm
40
CF
FRONT
CUT 1 ON FOLD
FOLD
29
32
32
CB
38.5
BACK
CUT 2
27.5

Shoulder bag

These cloth bags originated with the Bedouin, who rolled their belongings in the carpets from their tents when on the move. The modern version has been familiar to soldiers since the American Civil War. The Swedish Army had regulations from before the First World War until the sixties about the way in which they were to be worn in relation to the ammunition belt and the rucksack. The army shoulder bag had a lining which buttoned in and could be removed for cleaning. Soldiers kept dry goods, cutlery and sometimes even a saucepan in it. It was also useful for carrying hand grenades. It has now been replaced by the modern combat kit with bags in front and at the back. For food and eating equipment there are plastic bags which are disposable or more easily cleaned.

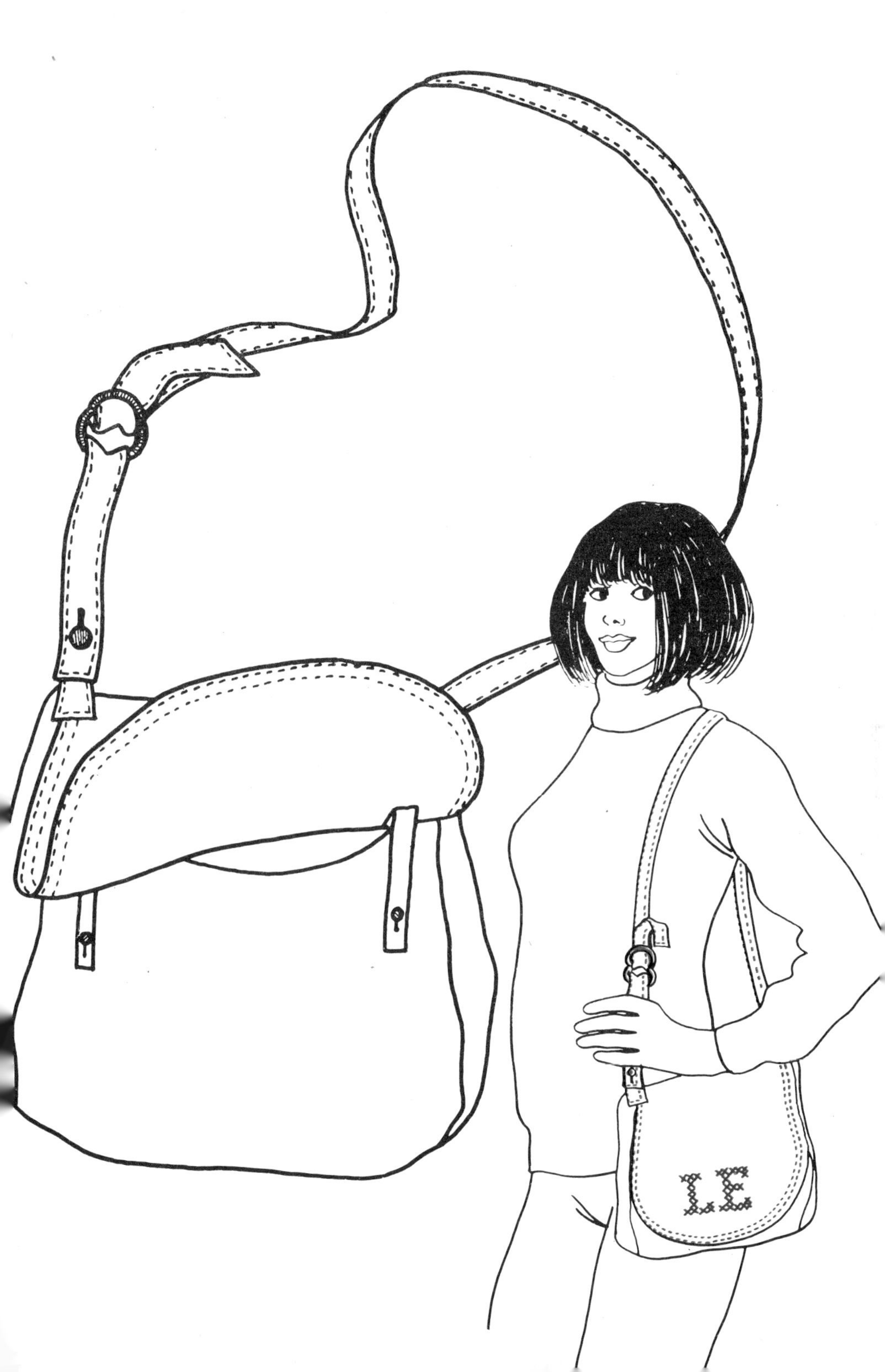
LE

Instructions
Shoulder bag

Material required: 100 × 90 cm; two rings; three buttons.
Seam allowance: 1 cm on all pieces.

Cut the bag from a double layer of cloth unless you are using canvas or other thick fabric. Lay the two flap pieces together, and sew round the long curved edge. Clip seams. Open out and press flat. Lay the body pieces (two thicknesses) right sides together and sew up the deep curve at the front. Clip seam. Turn and press.

Tack the side pieces to the body piece, right sides together. Sew and finish off the seam.

Sew the flap to the back with a fell seam. Press the flap. Make two rows of top-stitching round the edge of the flap 5 mm and 1·5 cm in from the edge.

Sew and turn the fastening straps and shoulder straps. Leave 3 cm open at one end of each of the shoulder straps. (Here the strap will be divided and sewn to the flap and the back separately.) Pin one leg of the shoulder strap to the body piece as marked on the pattern, and sew through both thicknesses; then pin the other leg to the flap and sew in the same way. For extra strength sew diagonally from corner to corner as well.

Attach the short shoulder strap on the other side in the same way. Make a buttonhole in the free end and sew on the button (see illustration). Fit two rings in the loop and thread the long shoulder strap through.

Make a buttonhole in each of the fastening straps and sew them to the underside of the flap. Sew buttons on the bag (see illustration).

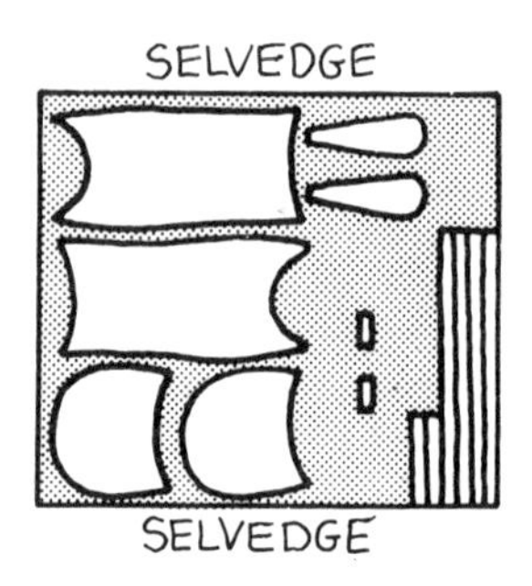

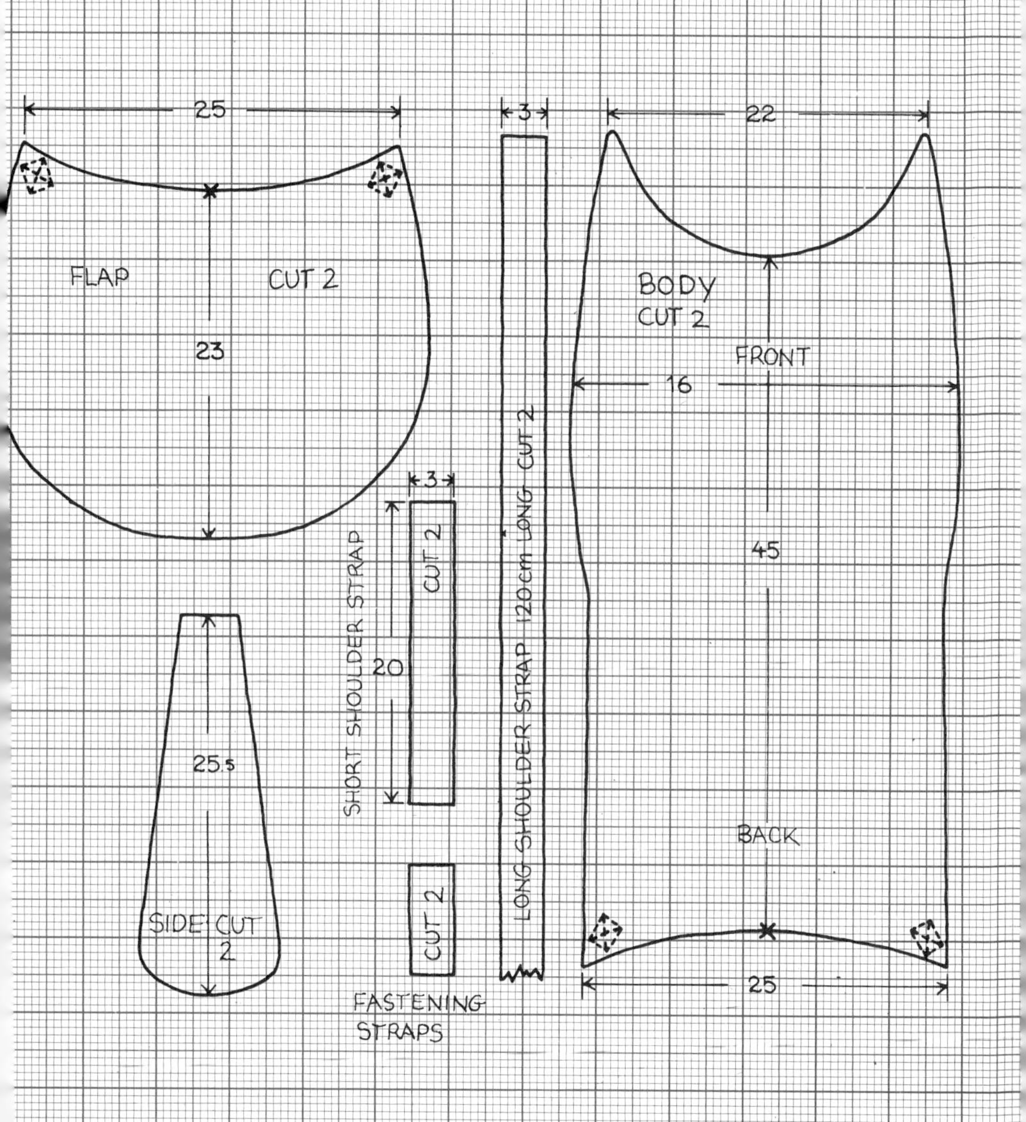
SCALE 1:5
25
FLAP
CUT 2
23
3
LONG SHOULDER STRAP 120cm LONG CUT 2
22
BODY
CUT 2
FRONT
16
45
BACK
25
3
SHORT SHOULDER STRAP
20
CUT 2
25.5
SIDE CUT 2
CUT 2
FASTENING STRAPS

Algerian dress

There is a particularly striking dress worn by Arab women in the villages near the Atlas mountains. It is almost full length and very roomy, cut with a yoke straight across the breast, from which it falls in soft pleats or gathers. The material is usually cotton with tiny, multicoloured flower prints. On top of this go eye-catching decorations in straight and scalloped braids of clear, strong colours.

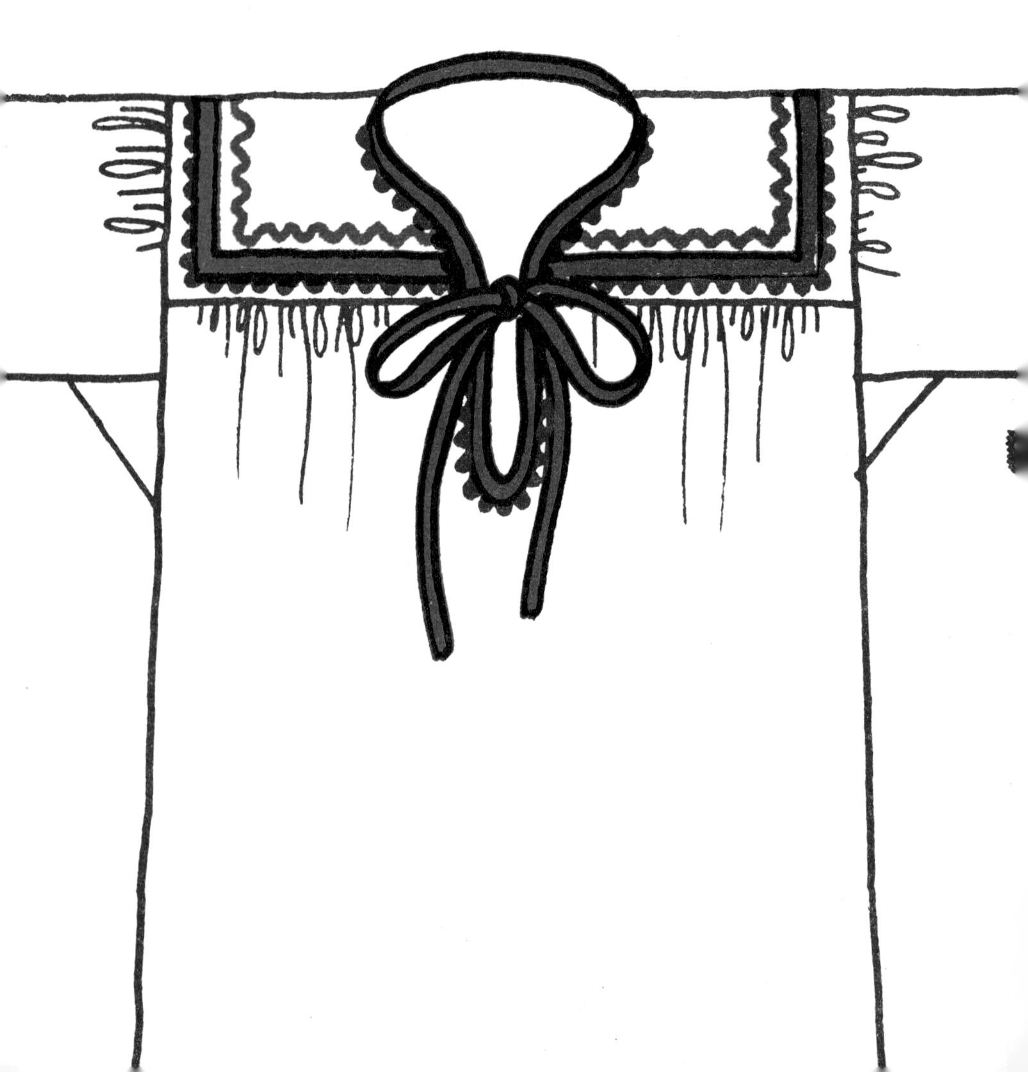

Instructions
Algerian dress

Material required: 425 × 90 cm; 300 cm bias binding; 420 cm rick-rack braid.
Seam allowance: 1 cm around all pieces; 4 cm at the hem.

Sew two gathering threads on the front and back pieces and at top and bottom of the sleeves. Gather front and back so that they fit the yoke. Lay the yoke on the front and back pieces, right sides together, and sew. Finish the seams.

Sew up the arms as far as the gusset marks. Finish the seams. Press.

Sew the wristbands, turn and press. Gather the sleeves to fit. Then lay one edge of the wristband right side down on the right side of the sleeve, and sew. Turn the wristband down, fold in the seam allowance and finish by hand on the inside.

Sew two sides of the gussets into the sleeves (see p. 17). Sew the side seams up to the gusset marks. Press open and finish the seams off.

Gather the tops of the sleeves into the yoke. Attach sleeves and gussets to the dress.

Bind the neck and front opening. Make ties, or a button and loop, for the opening. Hem the bottom by machine. Sew on the rick-rack braid for decoration. Press.

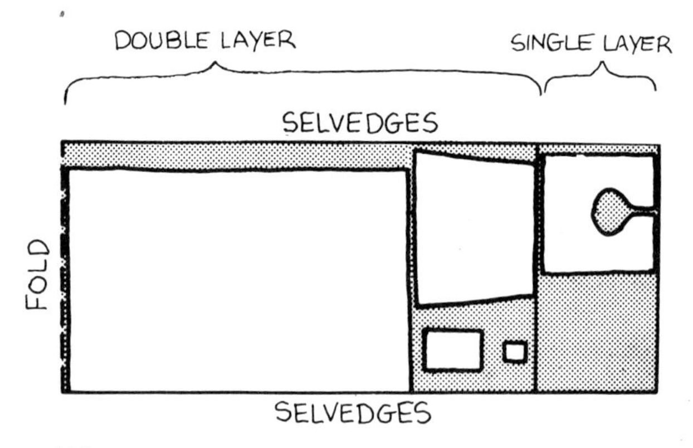

SCALE 1:10

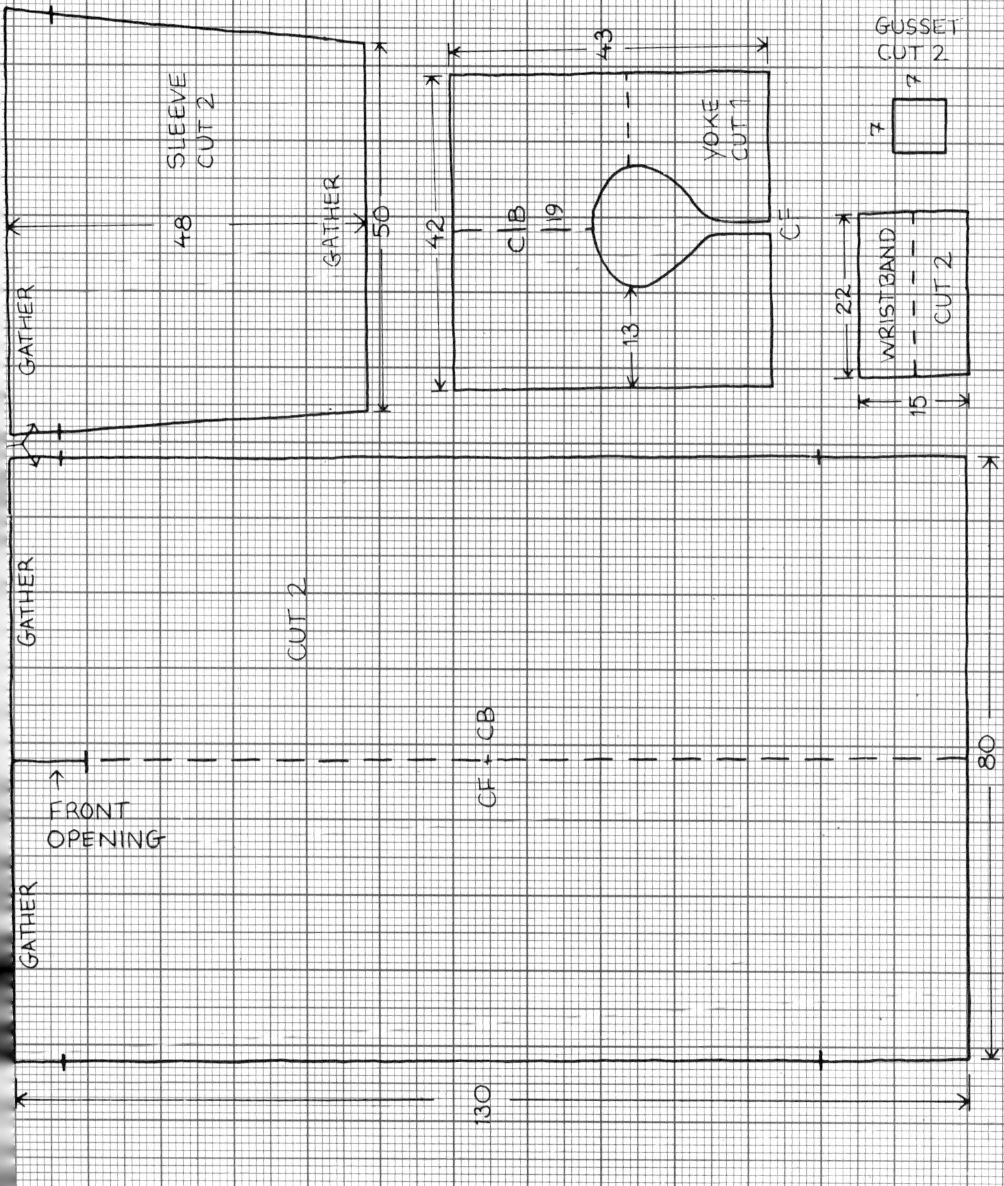

SLEEVE
CUT 2
48
GATHER
GATHER
50

43
42
C B
19
YOKE
CUT 1
CF
13

GUSSET
CUT 2
7
7

WRISTBAND
CUT 2
22
15

GATHER
CUT 2
CF + CB
80
FRONT
OPENING
GATHER
130

Fiddler's shirt

The so-called fiddler's shirt is one of the many forms of the shirt worn with folk costumes. The feature they have in common is that they are made out of the whole width of the material, sometimes with a shoulder seam or a yoke. They have straight sleeves with cuffs and either a collar or a neckband.

The collar is always a straight rectangular piece sewn to the neckline. In the 1800s it became high, decorated at its edges with embroidery, and was starched stiff so that it stood up to the ears. With this style a cravat was worn.

It was a custom that one extra fine shirt would be made that would never be worn; or rather it would be worn only on the wedding day and as a shroud.

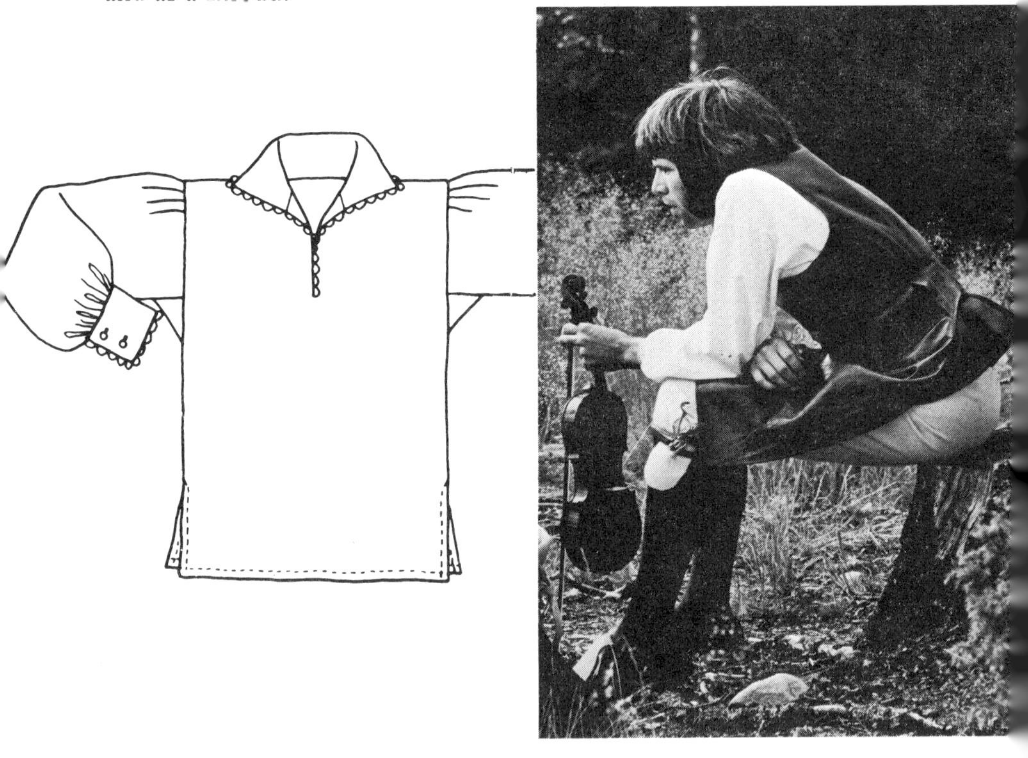

Instructions
Fiddler's shirt

Material required: 280 × 90 cm; 200 cm lace; four buttons.
Seam allowance: 1 cm around all parts, 3 cm at the hem.

Fold the collar and cuffs in two lengthwise and sew across the ends. Turn and press. Make the tucks at the top of the sleeves and tack firmly. Sew the sleeve seams from the gusset marks to the wrist openings. Turn under the seam allowance on the openings and hem. Sew two rows of gathering stitches at the bottom of each sleeve, and gather so that the sleeve fits the wristband. Pin to one edge of the wristband, right sides together, and sew. Turn to the inside, turn in the seam allowance on the wristband and slip-stitch over the seam. Sew two sides of the gusset to the sleeve (see p. 17).

Fold in a narrow turning on the neck opening and hem. Sew a 2 cm long dart below the opening for strength. Tack the collar to the right side of the shirt, right side down, centre-back marks matching. Sew. Clip the curved edge of the neck. Fold in the seam allowance on the collar and slip-stitch over the machine-stitching on the wrong side. Sew the side seams from the vents up to the gusset marks.

Make tucks at the top of the sleeves and tack firmly. Sew the sleeves to the body, putting an extra row of stitching round the gussets from the right side for strength.

Turn up the hem, and machine round it and the vents. Mark and sew buttonholes and buttons on the cuffs.

Attach lace round the collar, neck opening and cuffs either by hand or by machine. Press.

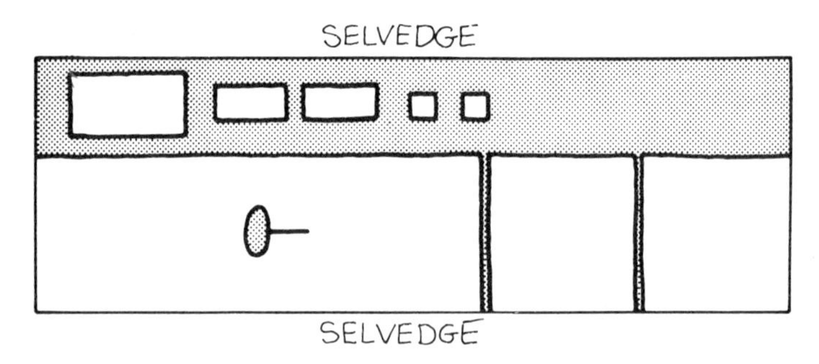

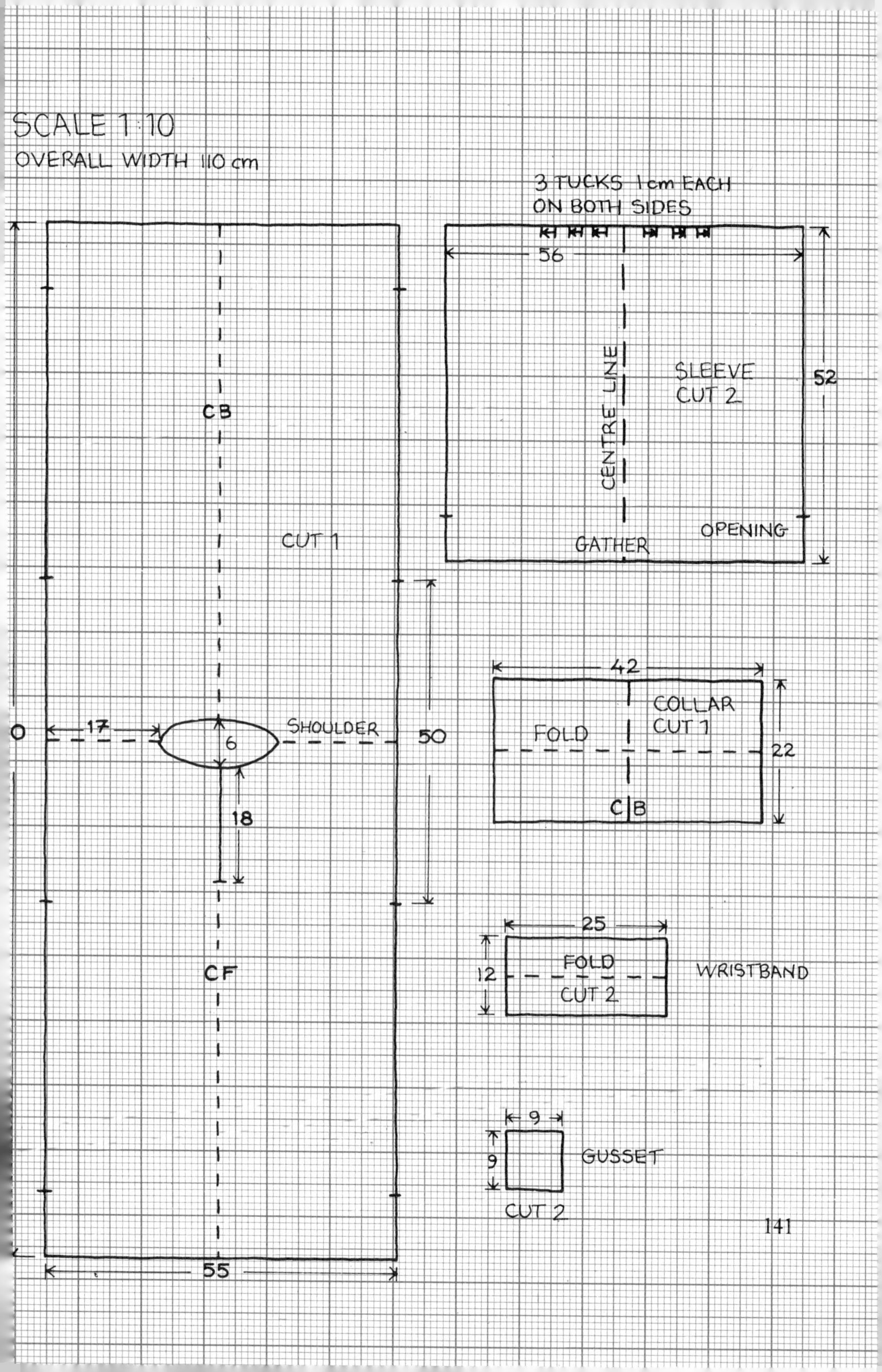
SCALE 1:10
OVERALL WIDTH 110 cm
3 TUCKS 1 cm EACH
ON BOTH SIDES
56
CENTRE LINE
SLEEVE
CUT 2
52
GATHER
OPENING
CB
CUT 1
O
17
6
SHOULDER
50
18
CF
55
42
COLLAR
CUT 1
FOLD
22
C B
25
FOLD
12
CUT 2
WRISTBAND
9
9
GUSSET
CUT 2

Apron (1880)

The apron was an important part of female servants' uniform from the 1880s right up to the Second World War, when servants became rare. For below-stairs work a dark, rough cotton was the rule; while the maids who moved amongst the finer folk in the drawing rooms upstairs had to wear a white or light-coloured apron.

As a piece of clothing the apron has a long history, full of changes. It is a functional garment in its own right; yet it can still be worn either for protection or for show, or both.

With a wide frill
With three tucks

With pockets and
rick-rack braid
With two frills
edged with bias
binding

Instructions
Apron (1880)

Material required: short apron, 85 × 90 cm; long apron, 125 × 90 cm. **Seam allowance**: 1 cm around waist, ties and waistband, 1·5 cm on the long side seams, 3 cm at the hem.

Sew the three panels of the apron together using fell seams for the long seams (see p. 15). Put in three horizontal tucks each 5 mm wide, at 3 cm intervals, starting 10 cm from the bottom. Hem the apron.

Hem the ties. Make a small tuck in the ends of the ties so that they will fit into the waistband, and attach them securely.

Gather or pleat the apron lightly at the waist. Tack it to the waistband, right sides together, and sew. Turn the waistband over and slipstitch on the inside. Press.

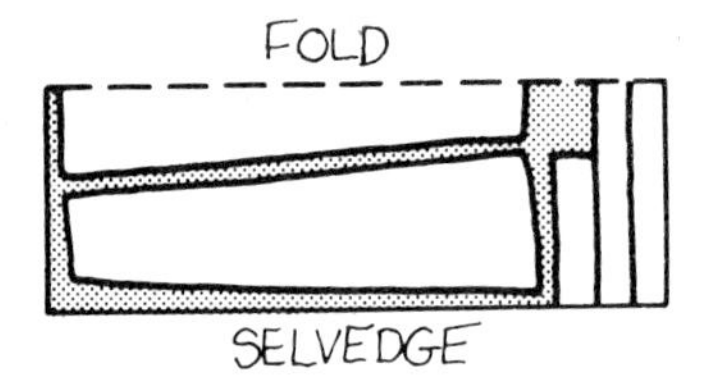

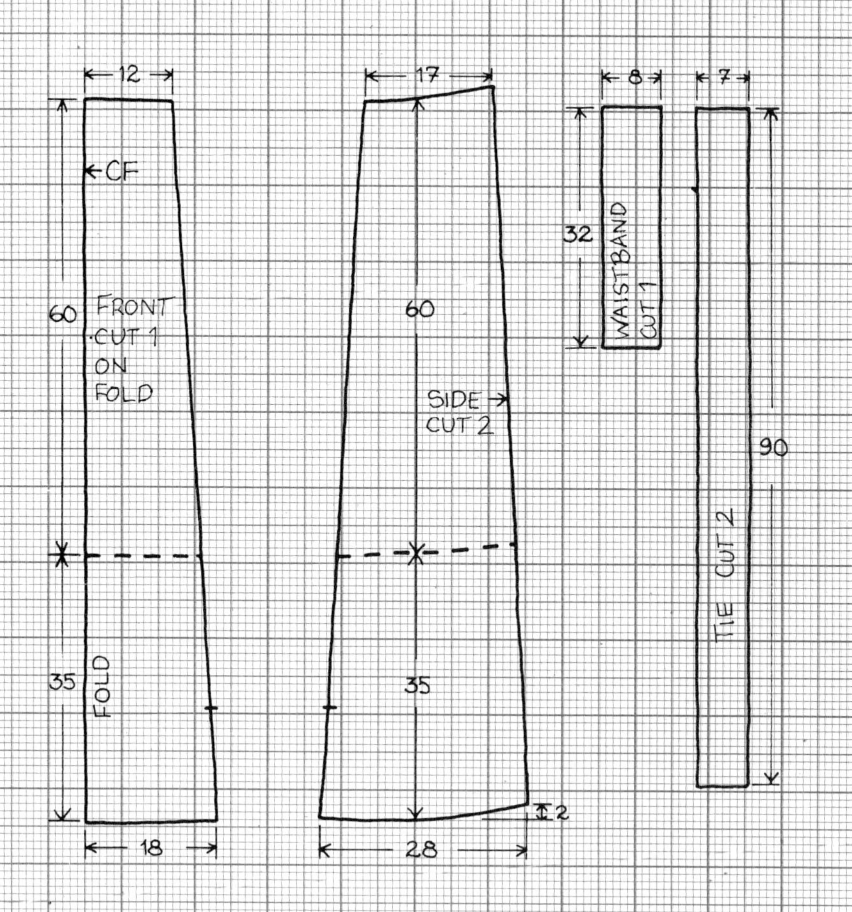

SCALE 1:10
12
CF
60
FRONT
CUT 1
ON
FOLD
35
FOLD
18
17
60
SIDE
CUT 2
35
28
2
8
32
WAISTBAND
CUT 1
7
90
TIE CUT 2

Child's pinafore

Around the turn of the century, simple pinafores in a variety of styles – striped, coloured, gingham – were a normal part of children's attire, whether boys or girls, from the toddler stage onwards. They are a familiar sight in pictures of the period. Girls were obliged to wear them at school; indeed a clean and freshly-ironed pinafore often had to hide the shortcomings of the clothes underneath.

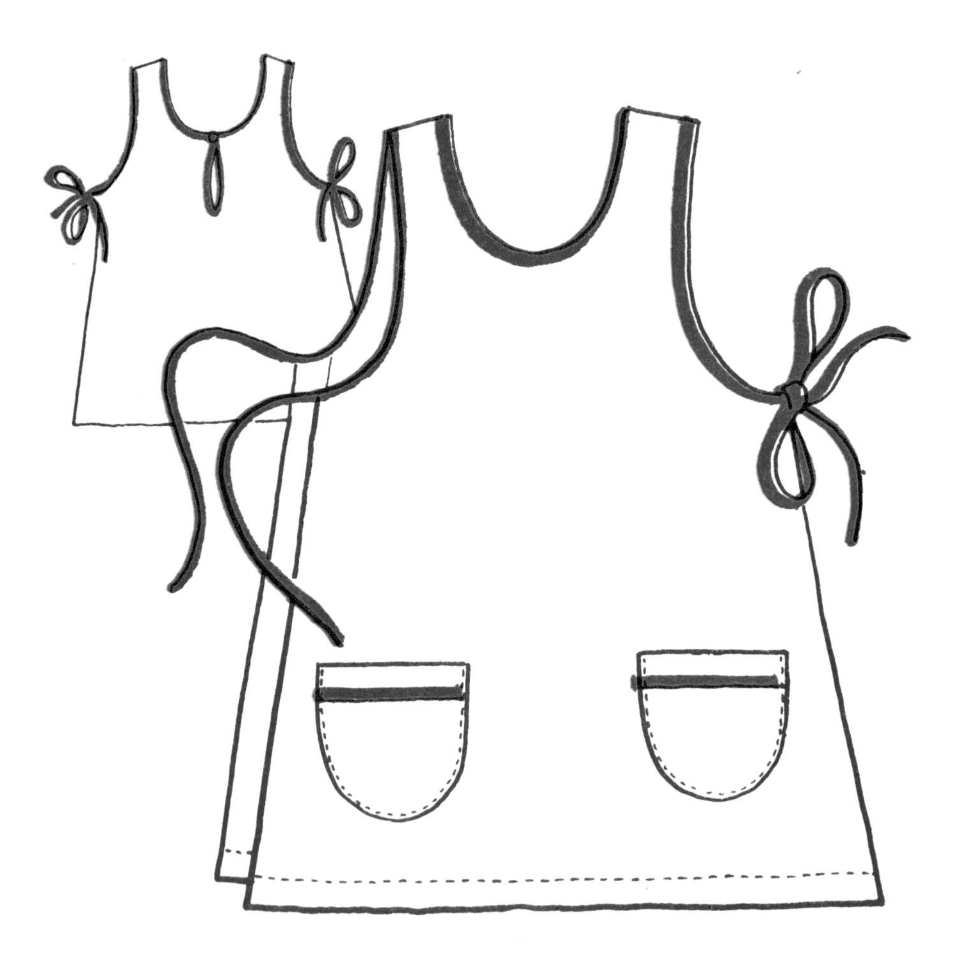

Instructions
Child's pinafore

Material required: 90 × 90 cm; 300 cm bias binding; one button.
Seam allowance: 2 cm on the sides, 3 cm at the hem.

Hem the tops of the pockets and press in the seam allowances all round. Sew bias binding on the right side for decoration. Sew on the pockets where shown. Press in the seam allowances on the sides of the apron and the hem, front and back, and sew.

Bind the back opening, the neck and the armholes, leaving enough binding free for ties. Alternatively, ties can be made from the material of the apron itself, sewn, turned and attached to the sides.

Sew button and loop on the back opening. Press.

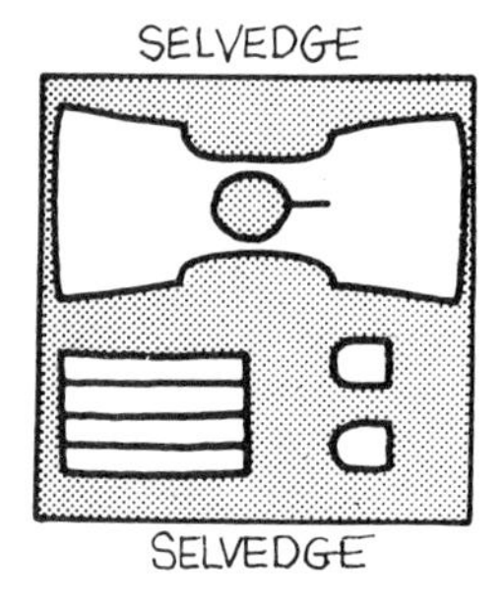

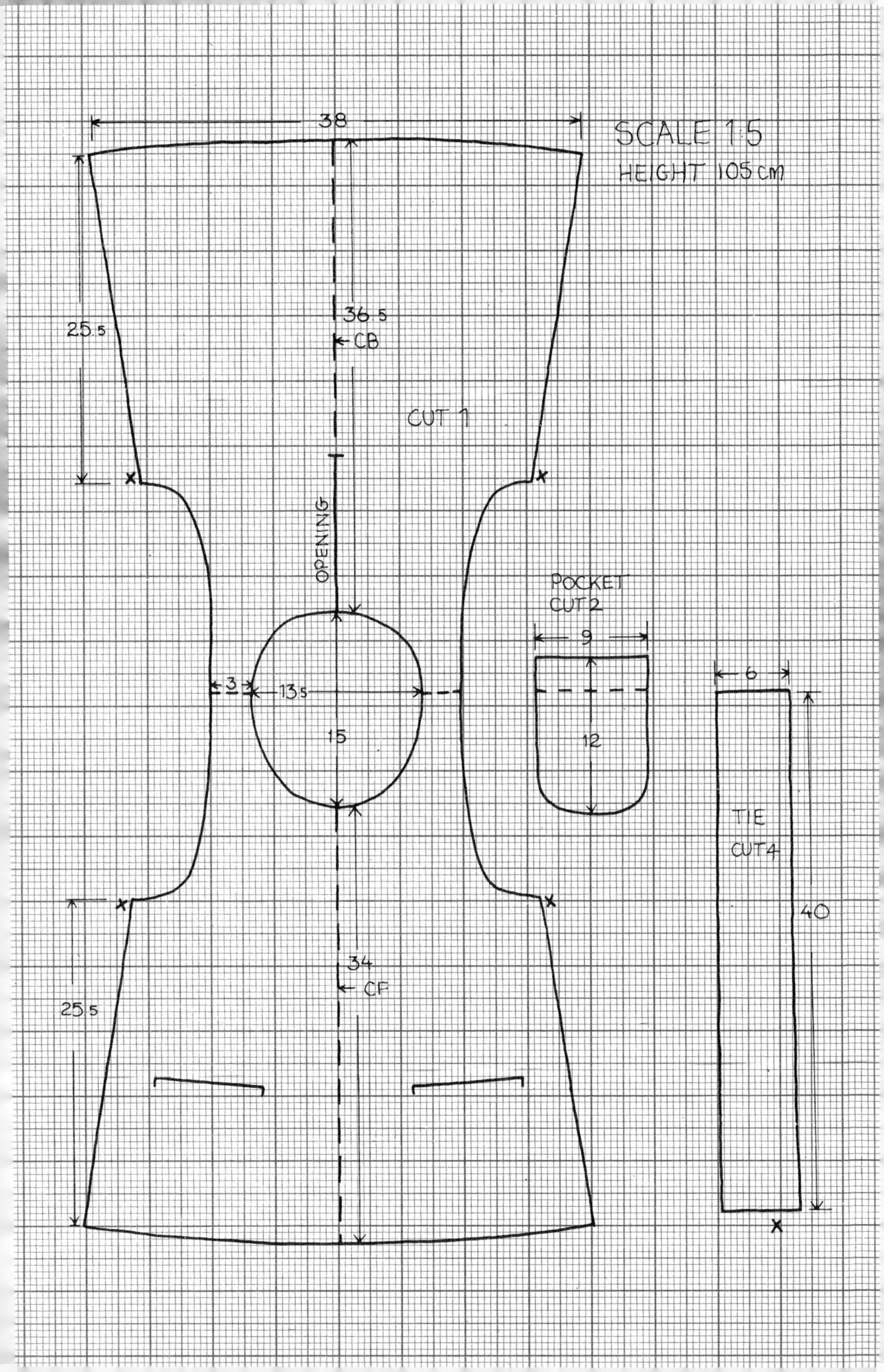

SCALE 1:5
HEIGHT 105 cm
38
25.5
36.5
CB
CUT 1
OPENING
3
13.5
15
34
CF
25.5
POCKET
CUT 2
9
12
6
TIE
CUT 4
40

Dirndl blouse

This blouse belongs to Austrian and Bavarian women's folk costumes. It is a gathered blouse of white cotton, and typically has short puff sleeves. Over it is worn a tight-fitting waistcoat which is quite often attached to a skirt so that the whole garment becomes a dress. The waistcoat and skirt are made out of different fabrics, and an apron is worn as well.

Instructions
Dirndl blouse

Material required: short-sleeved blouse, 200 × 90 cm; long-sleeved blouse, 275 × 90 cm; elastic for the sleeves; ribbon for the neck tie. **Seam allowance**: 7 mm round the neck, 12 mm around the sleeves and side seams, 3 cm at cuff and hem. Cut a small bias strip 3 × 5 cm for the buttonhole.

Sew the sleeves to the front and back with French seams, press. Sew the bias binding along the neckline, right sides together. Lay the small bias strip on the centre front at the top and sew 7 mm from the top edge. Turn it to the inside. Fold the bias binding out of the way, and sew two vertical buttonholes 2 cm apart through the blouse and bias strip as marked on the pattern.* Fold the bias binding to the inside and sew from the wrong side so that it makes a 12 mm casing.

Sew right up the side and sleeve seams with French seams. Fold under the wide hem of the sleeve and machine. Sew a second seam 12 mm in from the first to make a casing here too. Hem the blouse. Press.

Thread elastic in the sleeves and ribbon round the neck, pulling the ends through the buttonholes.

* The ribbon for the neck will be threaded through these buttonholes.

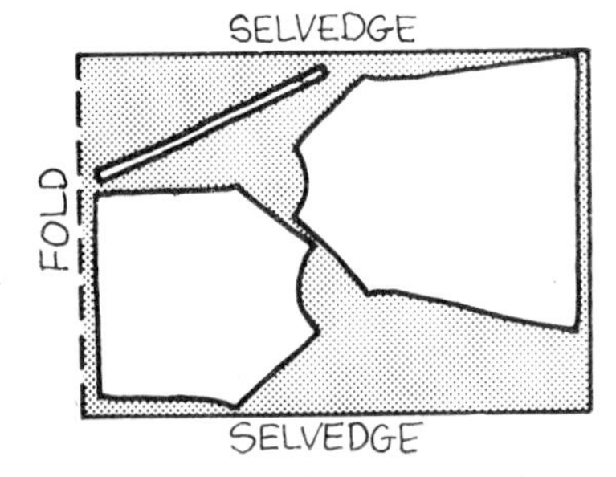

SCALE 1:10

WIDTH 104 cm
CENTRE-BACK LENGTH 52 cm

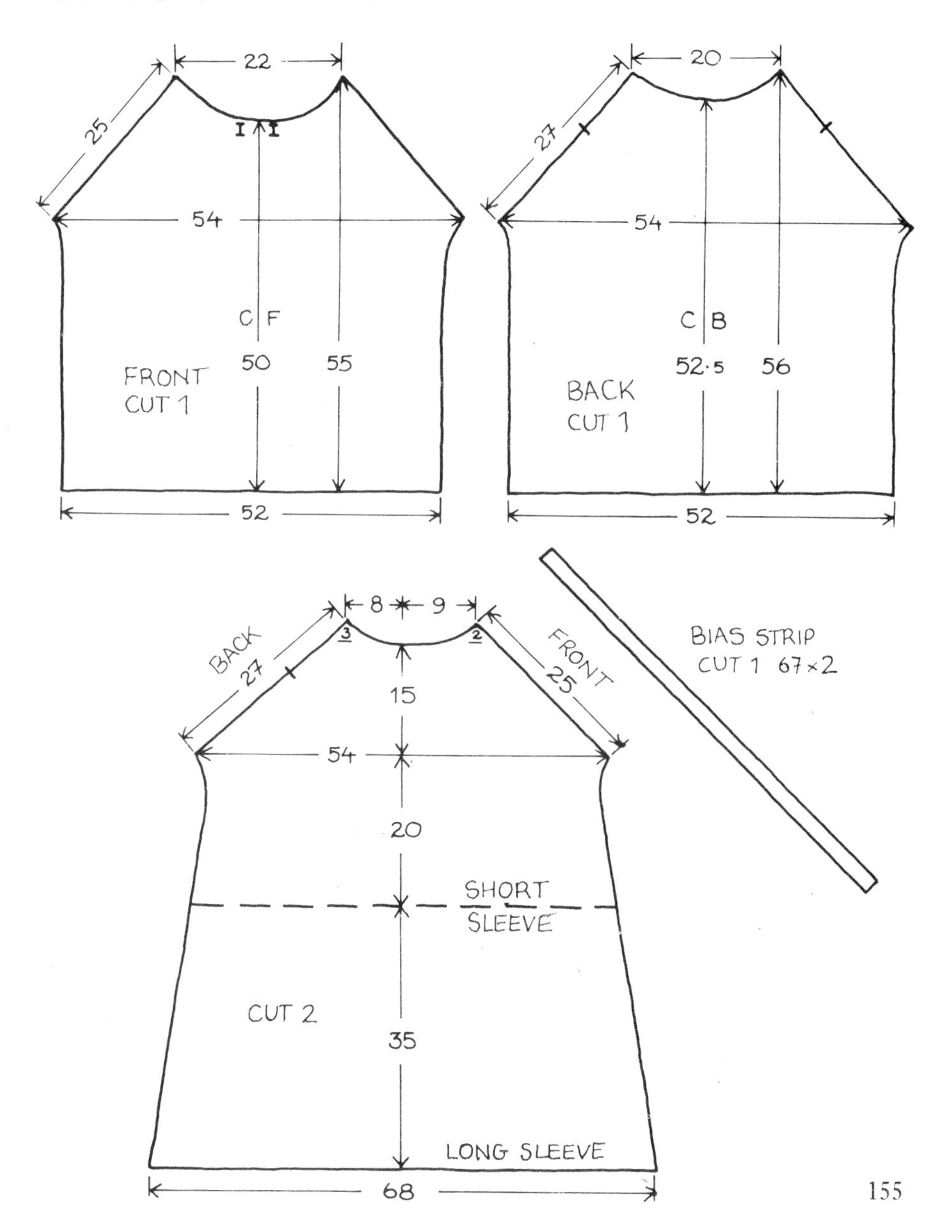

Blacksmith's shirt

Swedish blacksmiths and foundry workers in the nineteenth century used to wear a working shirt made from a single piece of cloth with a hole for the head, straight sleeves, a small upright collar and a flap in front. Sometimes it had tight cuffs, sometimes not. There were almost always vents in the sides.

There could hardly be a simpler shirt, but when the material had been woven at home and the shirt sewn by hand, it still represented many hours' work, so like all clothes in those days it was worth endless mending and patching. The material would be rough shirting linen which softened after many washes. A cloth-covered button at the neck is a nice detail.

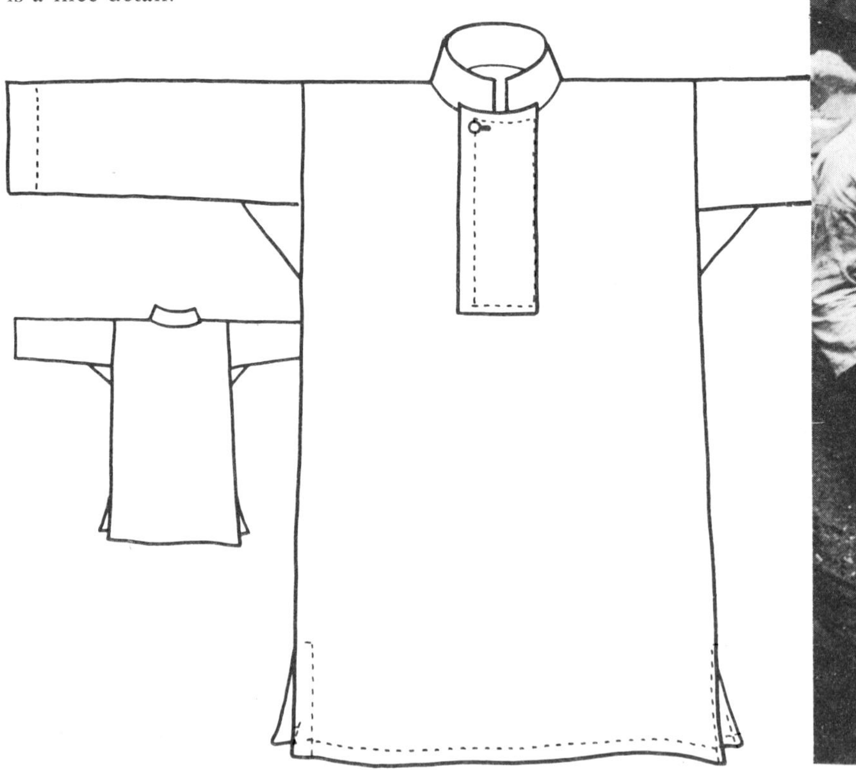

The shirt can be made as a tunic with belt and belt loops
Elasticate cuffs

Instructions
Blacksmith's shirt

Material required: 255 × 90 cm; one button.
Seam allowance: 1 cm around the neck opening and flap, 1·5 cm for the seams, 3 cm at the cuff and hem.

Lay facing directly over the neck opening, right sides together. Machine round the opening, slash, take a small nick out of the facing at the end of the cut, and turn it inside.

Sew and turn the neckband and flap. Press. Stitch the small tuck at the back of the neck. Lay the neckband right side down on right side of the shirt, with the centre-back marks matching. Tack to the shirt through a single layer of the neckband, sew, and turn up. Clip the seam. Fold in the seam allowance on the neckband and sew by hand on the inside of the shirt over the machined seam.

Attach one side of the gusset at the top of the sleeve seam (see p. 17); sew the sleeve seam and other side of the gusset in one go. Finish off seams, press open. Sew the side seams from the gusset marks to the vent. Finish the seams and press open. Tack in the sleeve with gusset attached; sew. Stitch round the gusset from the right side for extra strength. Turn up the hem and sew. Hem the vents. Hem the sleeves.

Top-stitch right round the front flap, tack it on, centred on the opening, and sew it to the shirt down one edge and across the bottom. Make a buttonhole in the flap at the neck and sew a button on the shirt. Press.

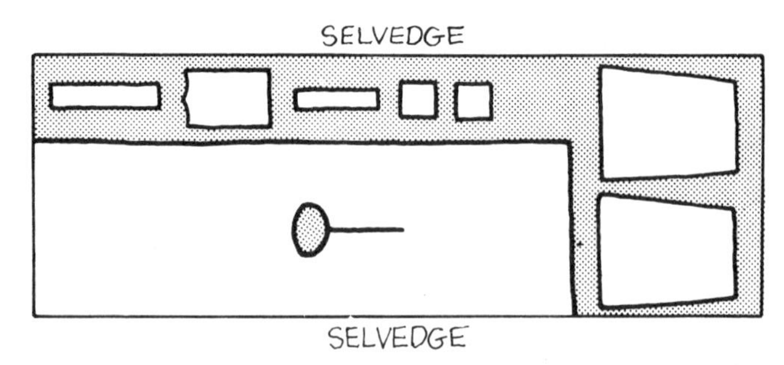

SCALE 1:10

CENTRE-BACK LENGTH 92 cm
WIDTH 120 cm

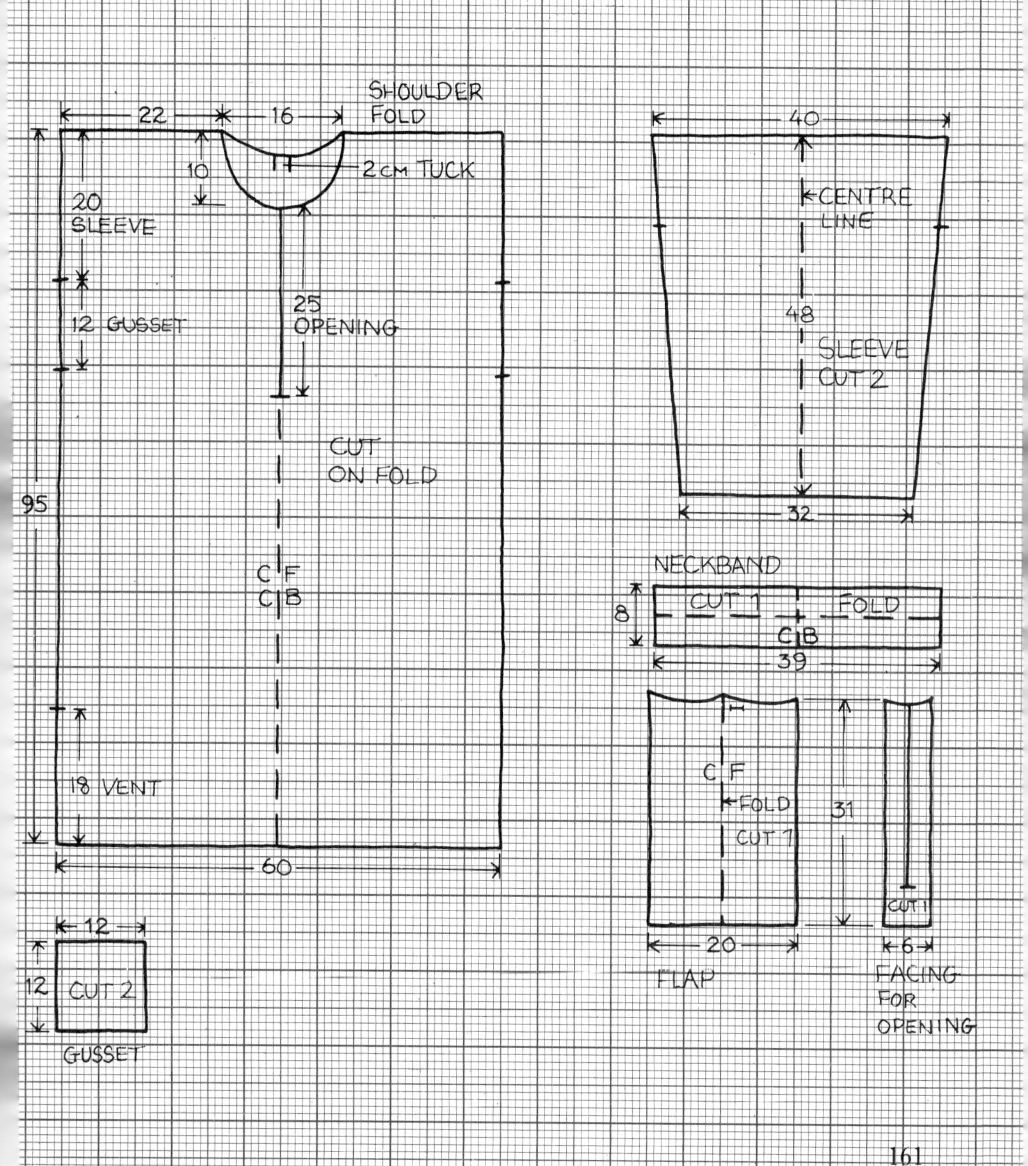

Wrap-around skirt

This is a more economical and better fitting version of the original wrap-round skirt. The oldest form of the garment is of course the kilt; and its great advantage is that it allows real freedom of movement, and its size is adjustable.

Instructions
Wrap-around skirt

Material required: short skirt, 135 × 90 cm; 380 cm bias binding; long skirt, 200 × 90 cm; 625 cm bias binding.
Seam allowance: 2 cm on the sides and at the centre back.

Sew the darts. Sew side and centre-back seams. Finish the seams. Press. Bind the skirt, starting with the front edge from top to bottom, and continuing all along the bottom and up the other edge. Bind the waist and leave a length of binding free at both ends for ties, 30 cm on the right front and 100 cm on the left.

Make a buttonhole in the right side seam just below the binding on the waist. Pull the long tie through that, bring it right round the back and tie on the left side. Press.

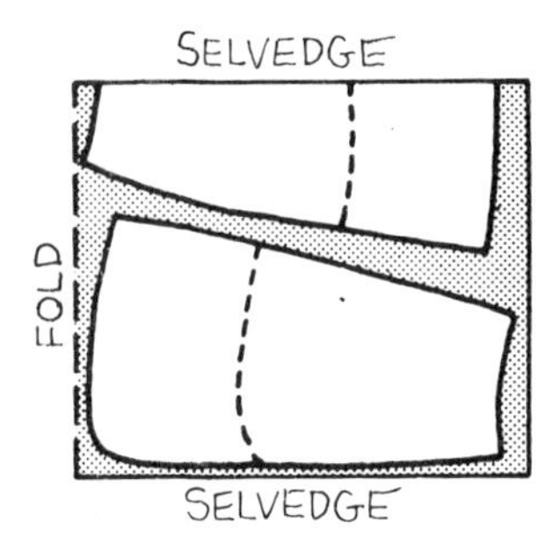

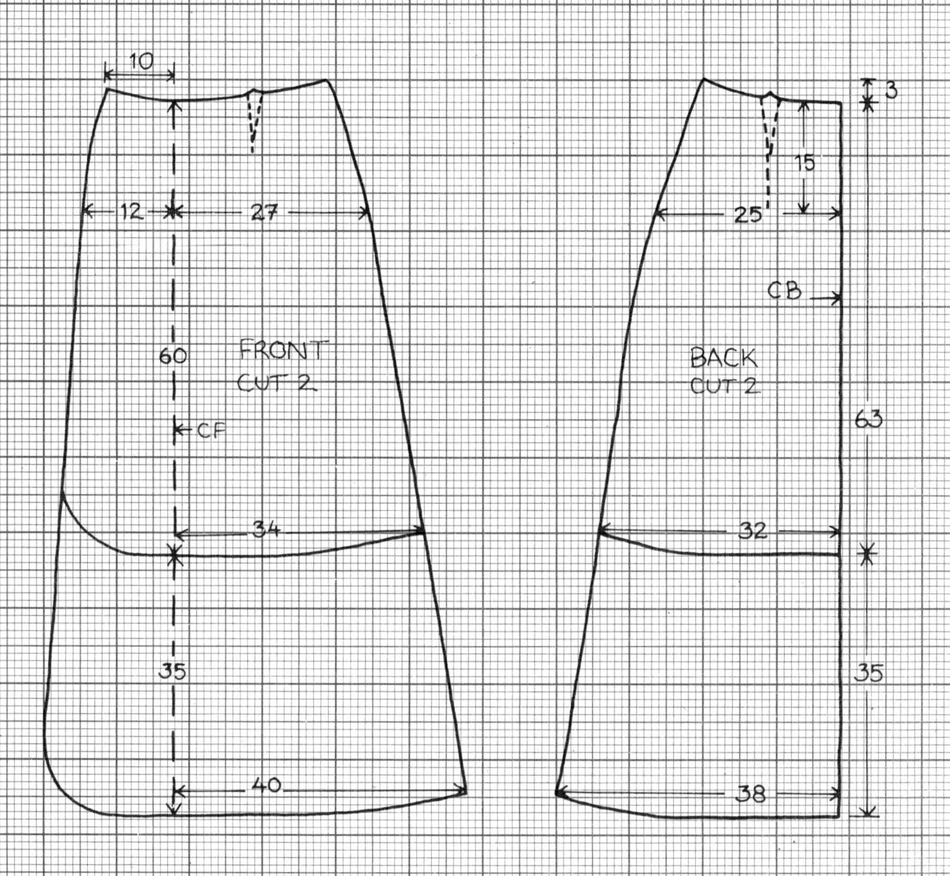
SCALE 1:10
WAIST 73 cm
10
12
27
60
FRONT
CUT 2
CF
34
35
40
3
15
25
CB
BACK
CUT 2
63
32
35
38

Dressing jacket

This garment was originally used by ladies to protect their clothes when brushing their long hair, powdering their faces and so on. Fashionable ladies in the early 1900s used to spend a great deal of imagination and inventive needlework on making different versions of the garment; one of these has survived as the hairdresser's overall. It is a pretty garment which could become fashionable again, with new and much wider uses.

Instructions
Dressing jacket

Material required: 250 × 90 cm; 450 cm lace.
Seam allowance: 12 mm at centre back, arm and side seams.

Mark and sew pleats. Fasten off the thread securely. Press the two pleats at the centre back towards the centre and press the rest outwards (see the illustration).

Sew sleeve and side seams in one with French seams. Sew up centre-back seam. Finish the seam unless you have used the selvedge. Press open. Oversew round the whole garment, sleeves as well, or make a narrow hem on the right side. Tack lace over this hem and sew. Press.

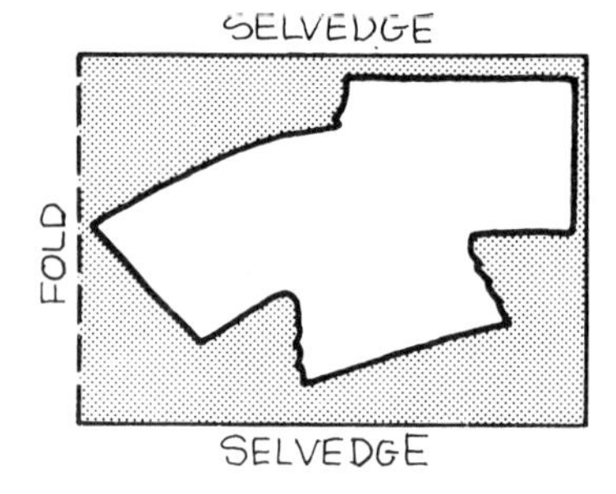

SCALE 1:10

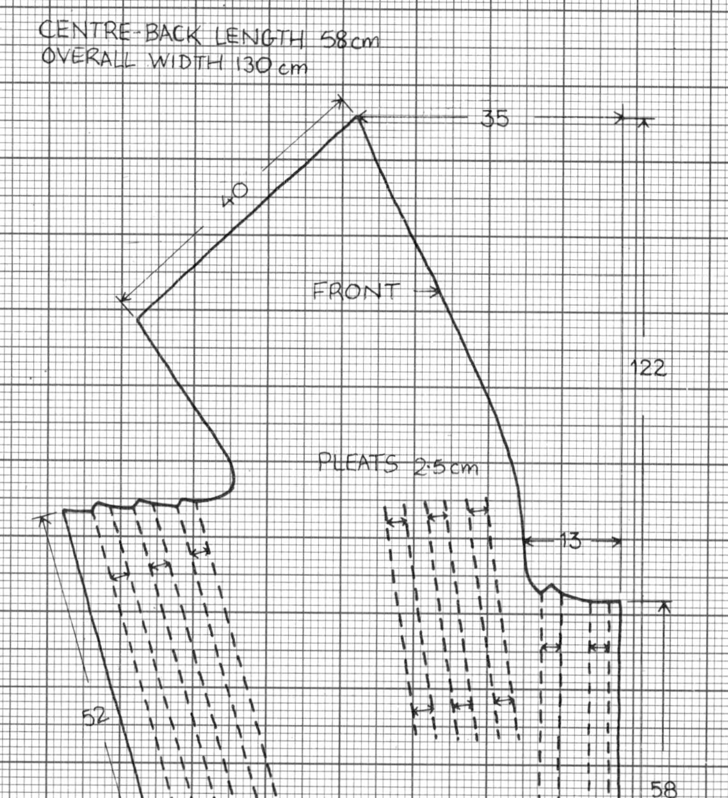

CENTRE-BACK LENGTH 58 cm
OVERALL WIDTH 130 cm
35
40
FRONT
122
PLEATS 2·5 cm
13
52
58
CUT 2
CB
39

Clothes sizes

Women

UK*	Continental	US
10	34	8
12	36–38	10
14	40–42	12
16	44–46	14

Men

UK and US	Continental
36	46
38–40	48–50
42–44	52–54
46–48	56–58

* See table on p. 11 for the measurements which correspond to these sizes.

Metric and imperial measurements – approximate equivalents

10 mm = 1 cm, 10 cm = 1 m

Imperial	Metric
½ in.	12 mm
1 in.	2·5 cm
12 ins.	30 cm
36 ins.	91 cm
45 ins.	114 cm
54 ins.	137 cm

Metric	Imperial
1 cm	just under ½ in.
12 mm	½ in.
2 cm	¾ in.
3 cm	1¼ ins.
4 cm	1½ ins.
5 cm	2 ins.
10 cm	4 ins.
50 cm	20 ins.
90 cm	35 ins.
1 metre	39 ins.
1 m 40 cm	55 ins.

More About Penguins and Pelicans

The Pauper's Homemaking Book

Jocasta Innes

The Pauper's Homemaking Book is concerned chiefly with the pleasure to be found in creating – with the cheapest of materials and tools – a home of one's own. Jocasta Innes's book is directed towards those people who are setting up home in earnest, who have lots of ideas and energy, and – after paying out mortgage or rent – almost no cash.

The hard-up homemaker needs to know how to get hold of cheap dining-chairs, revamp old sofas, re-lay secondhand carpets, and what to do about the stairs. These are among the most pressing needs for which the author gives detailed do-it-yourself instructions and drawings. Then she moves on to the more exciting possibilities of colour and paint on walls and transforming junk furniture. Finally, when the basics are accomplished, there is a section on how to make creative and attractive additions to the home, in the form of patchwork and quilting, picture framing and lamp making.

There are dozens of ideas here for turning a garret, cottage or modern semi into a home. Jocasta Innes's suggestions are inventive and original, intended to make any environment cheerful and comfortable rather than merely habitable, and they are, above all, cheap.

Simple Knitting

Maj-Britt Engström

Knitting is *easy*.

Basically, all you need to know is how to cast on, knit plain and cast off – and these instructions and more are given in *Simple Knitting*.

Choose from any number of yarns, needles, colours and sizes and make your own sweaters, mittens, socks, scarves, shawls and ponchos.

Everybody's Knitting

Kirsten Hofstätter

A medley of assorted patterns for the whole family to knit.

Kirsten Hofstätter has included all sorts of ideas and variations for pullovers, hats, scarves and other items, and suggests a number of ways to liven up the garments with knitted-in fruits, flowers and animals.

The Penguin Book of Knitting

Pam Dawson

The Penguin Book of Knitting will be invaluable, both for the beginner and for the more experienced knitter.

Pam Dawson, of the BBC Television knitting series, has put together an expert guide to different stitches and techniques, together with an imaginative selection of patterns for men, women, children and babies.